外贸商函 提分宝典

WAIMAO SHANGHAN
TIFEN BAODIAN

真题

张会忠　主编

浙江工商大学出版社
ZHEJIANG GONGSHANG UNIVERSITY PRESS

· 杭州 ·

图书在版编目(CIP)数据

外贸商函提分宝典 / 张会忠编. —杭州:浙江工
商大学出版社,2021.9(2022.10重印)
ISBN 978-7-5178-4647-5

Ⅰ. ①外… Ⅱ. ①张… Ⅲ. ①对外贸易—电报信函—
写作—高等职业教育—入学考试–自学参考资料 Ⅳ.
①F75

中国版本图书馆 CIP 数据核字(2021)第169541号

外贸商函提分宝典
WAIMAO SHANGHAN TIFEN BAODIAN
张会忠 主编

责任编辑	李远东
封面设计	沈 婷
责任印制	包建辉
出版发行	浙江工商大学出版社
	(杭州市教工路198号 邮政编码310012)
	(E-mail:zjgsupress@163.com)
	(网址:http://www.zjgsupress.com)
	电话:0571-88904980,88831806(传真)
排 版	杭州朝曦图文设计有限公司
印 刷	广东虎彩云印刷有限公司绍兴分公司
开 本	889mm×1194mm 1/16
印 张	10
字 数	277千
版 印 次	2021年9月第1版 2022年10月第2次印刷
书 号	ISBN 978-7-5178-4647-5
定 价	36.00元

 前 言

    高等职业教育作为职业教育的重要组成部分,为国家输送高技能人才、促进地方经济发展做出了重要贡献。在《中国教育现代化2035》的引领下,国家将加快发展现代职业教育,不断优化职业教育的结构与布局。

    作为外贸大省,浙江省内多所中职学校开设了外贸专业,且每年参加高职考试的学生数量比较稳定。同时,在浙江省高等职业教育考试中外贸类专业考试已实施多年且日趋成熟,但目前市面上的一些外贸商函复习类书籍没有明确的知识体系,结构松散,不太适合作为学生复习冲刺的教材。

    《外贸商函提分宝典》以最新的《浙江省高校招生职业技能考试大纲(外贸类理论知识)》为依据,以最近10年的高职考试真题为蓝本,将内容分为单词、词缀、词组、常用句子、语法和商函写作6个部分。本书内容翔实,体系清晰,使学生可学、能学、会学。

    本书在编写中充分考虑学生实际,有以下3个明显特点:

    1. 知识系统化,要求明确化。从基础字词到语句篇章,逐层递进,符合实际。

    2. 考试真题和巩固能力题相结合,有梯度和层次,全面帮助学生复习提升。

    3. 创新复习类书本结构,设置"学习点拨"和"知识加油站"两个部分,便于学生理解和拓展。

    在本书编写过程中,我们得到了宁波外事学校的鼎力支持,试用了该书部分章节的外贸专业课程教师和学生给予了积极反馈。同时,我们参考了闫兴伯、黄宪西的《商务英语函电(第二版)》,徐宝良的《外贸商函》以及于丽娟的《外贸商函(第二版)》等浙江省近10年来使用的中职外贸商函教材,同时借鉴了很多外贸商函相关书籍和网络资料,也得到了来自一线带考教师的宝贵意见,在此向他们表示由衷的感谢。

    由于时间仓促、编者能力水平有限,书中难免存在不足之处,恳请读者批评指正。

编 者

2021年4月

目 录

▶ 单词篇

一、单词拼写

(一) 单词拼写错误

➤ **能力要求**

了解常见的单词拼写错误类型。

掌握易误拼单词的正确拼法。

➤ **知识储备**

1. 易误拼单词

正确拼法	常见错误拼法	单词含义	词组强化
acceptance	acceptence	接受,承兑	documents against **acceptance** (承兑交单)
article	artical	条款,货物	**Article** No. (货号)
available	avaliable	可以获得的, 可以得到的	be **available** for export (可供出口)
beneficiary	benificiary	受益人	applicant and **beneficiary** (申请人和受益人)
catalogue	catelogue	目录	illustrated **catalogue** (图解目录)
claim	cliam	索赔	settle a **claim** (理赔)
contact	contect	联系,联络	**contact** us (联系我们)
conveyance	conveyence	运输,运送	means of **conveyance** (运输工具)
confirmation	comfirmation	确认	final **confirmation** (最终确认)
commencement	comencement	开始	date of **commencement** (启运日期)

- 1 -

正确拼法	常见错误拼法	单词含义	词组强化
declare	declear	申报	customs declaration （报关，报关单）
delay	deley	耽搁，延误	without delay （毫不耽搁）
damage	demage	损坏	sustain damage （遭受损坏）
discrepancy	descrepancy	不符合	discrepancy and claim （异议与索赔）
description	discription	描述	description of goods （货物描述）
financial	finanical	财政的	financial risk （财务风险）
fulfill	fullfill	实现，履行	fulfill an order （履行订单）
foreseen	forseen	预见的	foreseen situation （可以预见的情况）
grateful	greatful	感激的	be grateful to sb. （向某人表达感谢）
handle	handl	经营，处理	handle garment （经营服装）
latest	lastest	最新的	the latest pattern （最新的款式）
material	meterial	材料	raw material （原材料）
partial	partical	分批的	partial shipment （分批装运）
pattern	patern	式样，款式	various patterns （款式多样）
purchase	perchase	采购，购买	purchase order （采购合同）
requirement	requirment	需求，需要	meet one's requirement （满足某人的要求）
recommend	recommand	推荐	strongly recommended goods （强烈推荐的产品）
relevant	relavent	有关的，相关的	relevant company （相关公司）
salable	sellable	可销售的，有销路的	be salable （畅销）
separate	seperate	单独的，分开的	by separate post （另行封寄）

续 表

正确拼法	常见错误拼法	单词含义	词组强化
survey	servey	调查	**survey** report （调查报告）
solve	slove	解决	**solve** the problem （解决问题）
status	statues	状况,地位	financial **status** （财务状况）
textile	taxtile	纺织品	home **textile** （家纺）
trial	trail	实验的	a **trial** order （尝试性订单）
valid	vaild	有效的	remain **valid** （保持有效）

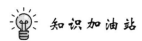 学习点拨

　　单词拼写错误一般是由于单词内部字母顺序交换(如 trail/trial)、字母不发音而导致漏写(如 therefore 中的 e)以及读音相近、相似或相同(如-ence/-ance)等造成的。

知识加油站

单词中不发音的字母

◎ gn 在一起且位于末尾时,g 通常不发音:

design　　　　　　　　foreign　　　　　　　　sign

◎ gh 在一起,通常不发音:

delight　　　　　　　　sight　　　　　　　　weight

◎ 两个相同字母在一起时,只发一个音:

apply　　　　　　　　commission　　　　　　　　illustrate

◎ 特殊情况:

exhibition(hi 不发音)　　receipt(p 不发音)

2.句子中的拼写错误

(1)动词变名词时变形混淆

①Please give us a definite assurance (assurence ×) of punctual shipment.

②At the beginning (begining ×) of this month, we shipped the goods.

③We need your sample cutting (cuting ×) for study.

④We need an explanation (explaination ×).

⑤Remittance（remitance ×）is commonly used in international trade.

⑥Please advance the date of shipment（shippment ×）to May 10.

（2）单词语法变形后字母漏写、多写

①As we're fully committed（commited ×）, we cannot accept the order.

②We demand a competitive（competive ×）price.

③Currently，the market is **declining**（decling ×）.

④Referring（Refering ×）to your email of Aug. 10, we're unable to accept the price.

⑤It's regrettable（regretable ×）that your offer is unrealistic.

⑥We're writing（writting ×）to enquire for your goods.

（3）读音相近或相同导致混淆

①The premium should be *borne*（born ×）by you.

②We *enclose*（inclose ×）you a copy of our catalog.

③The establishment of L/C will tie up our **funds**（founds ×）.

④We **owe**（own ×）your name to Bank of Ningbo.

⑤The new product **sells**（sales ×）well.

（4）字母不发音导致漏写

①Please do your best to enable us to catch the Christmas（chrismas ×）season.

②Your price is on the high side. Therefore（therefor ×）, there is no possibility of business.

③We will attend the exhibition（exbition ×）next week.

 学习点拨

句子中的单词拼写错误一般是由单词受语法规则变化**变形不正确、读音相近或相同导致混淆**以及**字母不发音导致漏写**造成的，日常学习中要留心。

 知识加油站

以 e 结尾的形容词变为副词的规则

◎ 一般情况下，直接加 ly：

complete—completely	definite—definitely	entire—entirely
extreme—extremely	immediate—immediately	late—lately
precise—precisely	respective—respectively	safe—safely
sincere—sincerely	unfortunate—unfortunately	wide—widely

◎ le 在末尾时，去 e 后加 y：

equitable—equitably	possible—possibly	simple—simply

（特殊情况：whole—wholly）

◎ 以 ue 结尾，去 e 加 ly：

due—duly	true—truly

(二)字形相似,意不同

➤ **能力要求**

区分并掌握函电考试中出现的拼写相似的词汇的含义。

➤ **知识储备**

(1)abroad vs aboard vs broad vs board

◇ abroad是副词,意为"在国外",常用词组 at home and abroad(国内外)。

◇ aboard是副词,意为"在甲板上",相当于 on board。

◇ broad是形容词,意为"宽广的",如 a broad range of goods(各种各样的产品)。

◇ board是名词,意为"甲板、木板",如 on board B/L(已装船提单)。

(2)cause vs clause

◇ cause是动词,意为"造成",如 cause us inconvenience(给我们造成不便)。

◇ clause是名词,意为"条款",如 amend a clause(修改条款)。

(3)compete vs complete

◇ compete是动词,意为"竞争",如 compete with others(同其他人竞争)。其名词为 competition,如 tough competition(竞争激烈)。

◇ complete作动词、形容词皆可。作动词时,意为"完成",如 complete delivery(交清货物)。作形容词时,意为"完全的",如 complete catalog(完整的目录)。

(4)confirm vs conform

◇ confirm是动词,意为"确认;保兑",如 confirm your order(确认你方订单),a confirmed L/C(保兑的信用证)。其名词为 confirmation,常用短语 sales confirmation(销售确认书)。

◇ conform是动词,意为"符合",如 conform to sth.(与……相一致)。其名词为 conformity,常用短语 in conformity to/with(依照)。

(5)contact vs contract

◇ contact作动词、名词皆可,意为"联络",它是及物动词,如 contact our supplier(联络我们的供应商),不用 with;作名词时,可以用 make contact with sb. 这一结构。

◇ contract是名词,意为"合同",如 sign a contract(签合同)。

(6)corporation vs cooperation

◇ corporation是名词,意为"公司",如 a leading corporation(大公司)。

◇ cooperation是名词,意为"合作",如 long-term cooperation(长期合作)。

(7)customer vs costumer vs custom vs customs

◇ customer是名词,意为"顾客",如 a valued customer(尊贵的客户)。

◇ costumer是名词,意为"服饰供应商",是在 costume(演出服)基础之上演变而来的。

◇ custom是名词,意为"风俗习惯",如 a traditional custom(传统习俗)。

◇ customs是名词,经常大写C字母,意为"海关",如 customs clearance(清关)。

(8)defect vs effect vs affect

◇ defect是名词,意为"缺陷、瑕疵"。其形容词为 defective,如 defective merchandise(残次品)。

◇ effect作动词、名词皆可。作动词时意为"实现、发生",如effect shipment(运输);作名词时意为"效应,效果",如take effect(生效)。

◇ affect是动词,意为"影响",如affect the cooperation(影响合作)。

(9)demand vs command vs recommend

◇ demand作动词、名词皆可,意为"要求、需求",如a strong demand(需求旺盛)。

◇ command作动词、名词皆可,意为"命令、控制",如command a good market(畅销)。

◇ recommend是动词,意为"推荐",如strongly recommended goods(强烈推荐的产品)。其名词为recommendation。

(10)exception vs expectation

◇ exception是名词,意为"例外、除外",如make an exception(破例一次)。

◇ expectation是名词,意为"期待",是expect的名词,如beyond our expectation(超出我方预期)。

(11)intend vs extend vs expand

◇ intend是动词,意为"打算",如intend to develop a new market(打算开拓新市场)。其名词为intention(意图,目的)。

◇ extend是动词,意为"扩展、延展",如extend insurance coverage(扩展保险范围)。其名词为extension。

◇ expand是动词,意为"扩大",如expand the business(扩大业务)。其名词为expansion。

(12)insure vs ensure vs assure

◇ insure是动词,意为"保险",如insure the goods(为货物投保)。其名词为insurance。

◇ ensure是动词,意为"确保",如ensure the safety of goods(请确保货物的安全)。

◇ assure是动词,意为"向……保证",如assure you of timely shipment(向你们保证及时交货)。

(13)later vs latter vs latest vs lately

◇ later是late的比较级,意为"稍后的,稍晚的",如call you later(晚点联系您)。

◇ latter是形容词,意为"(刚提及的两者中)后者的",常用句型"The former..., the latter..."(前者……,后者……)。

◇ latest是late的最高级,意为"最新的",如the latest style(最新的款式)。

◇ lately是副词,意为"最近",相当于recently。

(14)loose vs lose vs loss

◇ loose是形容词,意为"松散的",如loose package(散装)。

◇ lose是动词,意为"弄丢",如lose confidence(丧失信心)。

◇ loss是名词,意为"损失",如huge loss(巨大的损失)。

(15)origin vs original

◇ origin是名词,意为"起源,原产地",如certificate of origin(原产地证)。

◇ original作形容词、名词皆可,作形容词时,意为"原创的,原来的",如original price(原价);作名词时,意为"正本"如original policy(正本保单)。

(16)prefer vs refer vs defer vs infer

◇ prefer是动词,意为"更喜欢",如prefer A to B(较之B,更喜欢A)。其名词为preference。

◇ refer是动词,意为"提及",如refer to sb.(向某人查询)。其名词为reference。

◇ defer是动词,意为"推迟,拖延",如deferred payment(延期付款)。

◇ infer是动词,意为"推断",如infer from...(由……推断)。

（17）rise vs raise vs arise

◇ rise是不及物动词,意为"上涨",如"The price rises by 5%."（价格上涨了5%）；也可以作名词,如a rise in price（价格上涨）。其动词变化为：rise—rose—risen。

◇ raise是及物动词,意为"上涨",如We will raise the price by 5%（我们将涨价5%）。其动词变化为：raise—raised—raised。

◇ arise是不及物动词,不能直接加宾语,意为"出现",常和from一起连用,意为"产生于、起因于",如The loss arose from your carelessness（损失是你们粗心造成的）。其动词变化为：arise—arose—arisen。

（18）though vs thought vs thorough vs through

◇ though是连词,意为"虽然、尽管",等同于although,不和but连用。

◇ thought是名词,意为"想法",如a careful thought（仔细考虑）。它也是think的过去式和过去分词。

◇ thorough是形容词,意为"彻底的",如a thorough investigation（彻底的调查）。其副词为thoroughly。

◇ through是介词,意为"通过",如open an L/C through a bank（通过银行开立信用证）。

 学习点拨

平时,可以运用**词形联想法**、**字母含义法**或**谐音记忆法**等对拼写相近单词进行区分。同时,要在语境中反复操练强化,方能掌握。

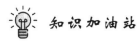 **知识加油站**

函电中经常以复数形式出现的词和短语

goods 产品	proceeds 所得款,收入
specifications 规格	thanks 感谢,谢谢
under the circumstances 在这种情况下	Ocean Marine Cargo Clauses 海运货物保险条款
shipping documents 运输单据	documents against acceptance 承兑交单
documents against payment 付款交单	as follows 如下
shipping instructions 装船指示	shipping marks 运输标志,唛头
in large quantities 大量	business relations 业务关系
as regards 关于,至于	best regards 真挚的问候
All Risks 一切险	sales contract 销售合同
terms and conditions 条件,条款	terms of payment 支付方式
thanks to 幸亏,由于	

（三）拼写有别,词相同

➤ **能力要求**

掌握商函考试中常见的有两种拼写形式的商函词汇。

➤ **知识储备**

(1)有"u"无"u"一个样(实际书写中,去u情况较普遍)

favour = favor   honour = honor   labour = labor

(2)"er/re"末尾换位不要紧

center = centre   meter = metre   liter = litre

(3)去尾简化容易记

catalogue = catalog   examination = exam   memorandum = memo

(4)特殊情况要牢记

check* = cheque(支票)   inquiry = enquiry   license = licence

(*当check为美式英语时,意为支票。)

 学习点拨

单词拼写略有不同主要受制于以下因素:美式英语与英式英语的区别、拼写简化趋势、特殊情况等。目前,美式拼写法更为大众所接受。

 知识加油站

英式英语与美式英语在拼写上的其他区别

英式英语	实例	美式英语	实例
-ise；-s-	realise；organisation	-ize；- z-	realize；organization
-ll	counsellor	-l	counselor
动词变形加 t	dreamt；learnt	动词变形加 ed	dreamed；learned

巩固与提升

[真题在线]

一、词语互译

1. 销售合同(2011年第78题)

2. survey agent(2011年第80题)

3. business contract(2012年第83题)

4. 合同(2013年第75题)

5. insurance policy(2014年第83题)

6. 投保金额(2015年第43题)

7. declaration of shipment（2015年第48题）　　8. 投保单（2017年第40题）

9. financial status（2018年第44题）　　　　10. be fully committed（2019年第46题）

二、句子翻译

1. 请将装运日期和信用证的有效期分别延长到7月5日和7月20日。（2012年第87题）

2. We are looking forward to getting some explanation for this delay.（2012年第94题）

3. We appreciate your cooperation and look forward to receiving your further order.（2013年第92题）

4. 合同规定以你方为受益人的信用证已通过中国银行宁波分行开立。（2015年第56题写作）

5. Without your specific request for insurance, we have insured the ordered goods against WPA for 110% of the invoice value.（2016年第54题写作）

6. 我们保证即期装运。（2016年第56题写作）

[强化练习]

一、词组互译

1. 图解目录　　　　　　　　　　　　2. 具体询盘

3. 出口许可证　　　　　　　　　　　4. 尝试性订单

5. 财务状况　　　　　　　　　　　　6. 劳动力成本

7. 毫不耽搁　　　　　　　　　　　　8. 装船指示

二、选词填空

1. ABC Trading Co. is doing business with clients at home and _____.（abroad/aboard）

2. Please _____ the goods against WPA.（ensure/insure）

3. We will _____ our price by 5% from Oct. 1.（raise/rise）

4. In view of our good relation, we are making you a _____ offer.（specific/special）

5. We _____ to expand our business in African market.（intend/extend）

6. Please sign the sales _____.（contact/contract）

7. The _____ in payment is for this transaction only.（expectation/exception）

8. We hope you can _____ us with a more favorable price.（recommend/accommodate）

三、单项选择题

1. Our customers _____ that payment be effected by D/P.

    A. expand   B. command   C. demand   D. extend

2. We hope to state that prices will _____ next month.

    A. rise   B. raise   C. arise   D. arouse

3. Please _____ the goods shall reach us in good time as stipulated.

    A. sure   B. ensure   C. assure   D. insure

4. We demand clean on _____ B/L.

    A. broad   B. abroad   C. board   D. aboard

5. We _____ having sold the following goods to you.

    A. inform   B. conform   C. confirm   D. form

6. It is regrettable that we have caused such huge _____.

    A. lose   B. loss   C. losing   D. loose

7. We are sure that such error won't _____ any more.

    A. occur   B. incur   C. cure   D. secure

8. Please note that our offer for Panda TV takes _____ since Oct. 1.

    A. affect   B. affective   C. effect   D. effective

四、句子翻译

1. 样品将另邮。

2. 如果有任何问题,请毫不犹豫地联系我们。

3. 海尔牌电器在国内外都很畅销。

4. 我们的最新报价在10天内有效。

5. 我们保证货物会准时到达目的港。

6. 关于付款,很抱歉目前不能满足你方的要求。

7. 请通过一家我们可以接受的银行开立一份以我方为受益人的信用证。

8. 很遗憾,我们不得不提价5%。

二、重点动词及拓展

► **能力要求**

掌握函电考试中重点动词的用法及其拓展情况。

► **知识储备**

1. appreciate

◇ 动词含义：感激

◇ 动词用法：

（1）appreciate + sth.

（2）appreciate + sb's doing sth.

常用句型：若蒙……，不胜感激。

（1）We shall appreciate it if...

（2）It shall be appreciated if...

◇ 拓展

（1）含义拓展

We appreciate the design of your goods.（我们**欣赏**你们产品的设计。）

The Euro is appreciating.（欧元在**升值**。）

（2）词性拓展

N.：appreciation

Adj.：appreciative

We're appreciative of your support.（感谢你方的支持。）

◇ 用法注意1：appreciate 作及物动词且表示"感激"时，其对象是事情。

We appreciate <u>you</u>.（×）　　　　We appreciate <u>your help</u>.（√）

◇ 用法注意2：不要把 appreciated 看成同 interested 等词一样而将其作表语，用于修饰人。

We are <u>appreciated</u> if...（×）　　　We are <u>appreciative</u> if...（√）

2. agree

◇ 动词含义：同意

◇ 动词用法：

（1）agree to do sth.

（2）agree with sb.vs agree to sth. vs agree on/upon sth.

In price，we don't agree with you.（同意，后面跟人）

We don't agree to your price.（同意，一方同意另一方，后面跟事物）

Both parties have agreed on/upon the price.（达成一致，主语一般是双方）

◇ 用法注意：agree 后面的 to 有两种情况：一种是不定式，意为"同意做某事"，如 agree to lower the price（同意降价），另一种是介词，后接名词，意为"同意某物"，如 agree to your proposal（同意你方的建议）。

— 11 —

◇ 拓展

（1）含义拓展

The stipulations of L/C should agree with those in the contract.（信用证条款应当与合同一致。）

（2）词性拓展

N.: agreement　　　　　　　They reached an agreement.（他们达成了一致。）

Adj.: agreeable　　　　　　Your price is not agreeable to us.（我们不同意你方的价格。）

3. assure

◇ 动词含义：保证，确保

◇ 动词用法：assure sb. of sth./that...

◇ 词性拓展：

N.: assurance

an assurance of prompt shipment（及时交货的保证）

常用句型：

Please rest/be assured that...（请放心，……）

4. compete

◇ 动词含义：同……竞争

◇ 动词用法：compete with

◇ 词性拓展

N.: competition　　　　　　tough/keen competition（激烈的市场竞争）

N.: competitor　　　　　　a competitor from Southeast Asia（来自东南亚的竞争对手）

Adj.: competitive　　　　　remain competitive（拥有竞争力的）

◇ 用法注意：compete 的名词 competition（竞争）同 competitive 的名词 competitiveness（竞争力）在意思上有明显区别，不要误用。

5. confirm

◇ 动词含义：确认；保兑

◇ 动词用法：confirm sth./doing sth./having done sth.

◇ 词性拓展

N.: confirmation　　　　　subject to our final confirmation（以我方最终确认为准）

Adj.: confirming　　　　　a confirming bank（保兑行）

Adj.: confirmed　　　　　a confirmed L/C（保兑信用证）

6. cover

◇ 动词含义：保险

◇ 动词用法：cover insurance on goods（为货物投保）

　　　　　　cover + 险别（投保××险）

　　　　　　have sth. covered（为某物投保）

◇ 拓展

（1）含义拓展

We have to adjust the price to cover the rising cost.（我们只得调价来弥补上涨的成本。）

Samples will be sent under separate cover.（样品另行封寄。）

（2）词性拓展

N.: cover   scope of cover = coverage(保险范围)

7. inform

◇ 动词含义:通知

◇ 动词用法:

（1）inform sb. of sth./sb. that...

◇ 词性拓展

N.: information   for one's information(供某人参考)

◇ 用法拓展:

keep sb. informed of sth.（informed作宾语补足语）

We will keep you informed of the details of shipment.（我们会告知装运细节。）

8. interest

◇ 动词含义:使……感兴趣

◇ 动词用法:sth. interest sb.（某物让人感兴趣）

◇ 词性拓展

N.: interest   We have interest in your products.

                      Your goods are of interest to us.

Adj.: interesting   Your goods are interesting（to us）.

Adj.: interested   We're interested in your products.

◇ 用法注意1:interesting是描述事物的,而interested是描述人的。

◇ 用法注意2:interest作名词,还可以表示利息,如interest rate(利率)。

9. regret

◇ 动词含义:遗憾

动词用法:regret to do sth./regret being unable to do sth.

◇ 常用句型:

（1）We very much regret to inform you that...(很遗憾告知……)

（2）We regret that...(很遗憾……)

（3）We regret our inability to do sth.（很遗憾我们不能做某事。）

◇ 词性拓展

N.: regret   Much to our regret, your price is on the high side.（很遗憾,你方价格偏高。）

Adj.: regretful   We're regretful that your price is unworkable.（很遗憾,你方价格行不通。）

Adj.: regrettable   It is regrettable that your price is too high.（很遗憾,你方价格太高。）

◇ 用法注意:regretful作表语时是描述人的,而regrettable作表语时是描述物或事情的,其副词形式为regrettably。regrettable在句子中还可以充当宾语补足语,如feel it regrettable(觉得此事很遗憾)。

10. request

◇ 动词含义:要求

◇ 动词用法:

（1）request（sb.）to do sth. 要求（某人）做某事

（2）A requests that B（should）do sth./sth.（should）be done（by B）（虚拟语气）

(3) as requested= at one's request(按照某人的要求)

◇ 词性拓展

N.: request   satisfy one's request(满足某人的要求)

11. satisfy

◇ 动词含义:使……满意

◇ 动词用法:sth. satisfies sb.(某物让人满意)

◇ 词性拓展

N.: satisfaction	We decide to repeat an order because of our satisfaction with your goods. (由于对你方产品满意,我们决定续订。)
Adj.: satisfying	We need a satisfying price.(作定语,满意的,多用于主观判断。)
Adj.: satisfied	We're satisfied with your products.(作表语,满意的,修饰人。)
Adj.: satisfactory	Your goods are satisfactory to us.(作表语,令人满意的,多用于事和物。)

 学习点拨

掌握一个实义动词需要把握三个方面:动词的**分类**(及物动词和不及物动词)、动词的**用法**(后接 to do sth. 或 doing sth.,固定短语,等等),以及它的**拓展**(其名词或演化出来的形容词、副词等)。

 知识加油站

很多单词兼具动词和名词两种词性。在实际运用中,我们经常会看到一些词性互换的情况。一般名词替代动词居多,但动词也可以进行具体化,充当名词。

抽象动词转换为具体名词

The imports sell well at our end. 进口的产品

Deliver us various makes of the sample. 式样,款式

We will try our best to meet your needs. 需求,需要

Once the supplies come in, we will contact you. 可供应的产品

巩固与提升

[真题在线]

一、单项选择题

1. Our customers are _____ with your goods.(2012年第61题)

    A. satisfactory   B. satisfy   C. satisfied   D. satisfaction

2. Please inform us _____ your terms of payment and send us samples.(2013年第60题)

A. of   B. on   C. to   D. in

3. We feel _____ that we have to adjust the prices. The new prices _____ on June 6, 2014. (2014年第65题)

    A. regretful, take effect   B. regret, take effect

    C. regret, will take effect   D. regretful, took effect

4. We _____ your quoting us your competitive prices on FOB Shanghai in the letter of Mar. 5th. (2016年第29题)

    A. appreciate it   B. will be appreciated

    C. are appreciated   D. appreciate

5. _____, we are sending you our latest samples of full-range garments. (2016年第32题)

    A. In your hope   B. With your requirement

    C. At your request   D. In need of

6. We _____ that it is _____ to accept your counter-offer. You may notice that the price for this item has gone up since last year. (2017年第34题)

    A. regret, possible   B. regret, impossible

    C. afraid, impossible   D. afraid, possible

二、句子翻译

1. 我方将以最有竞争力的价格满足贵方要求。(2011年第95题)

2. We appreciate your cooperation and look forward to receiving your further orders. (2013年第92题)

3. 你方对我们的报价也比较满意。(2013年第95题写作)

4. We trust that _____

    (贵方会对本次试订单满意的). (2014年第86题)

5. We decide to meet you halfway in your request for lower prices. (2016年第52题)

6. We propose to have the goods shipped in equal two lots. And please inform us whether you agree or not. (2017年第53题)

7. We have received your products we ordered, but we regret to say that they are very much inferior in quality to your samples. (2018年第53题)

8. 如对目录中所列之任何产品感兴趣,请具体询价。(2018年第56题)

[强化练习]

一、选词填空

1. We feel it _____ that your price is unworkable. (regretful/regrettable)

2. ABC Co. is _____ with our price and places an order. (satisfied/satisfactory)

3. Your price is too high to be _____. (acceptance/acceptable)

4. Our goods are salable because of their _____. (competitiveness/competition)

5. The seller requested that the L/C _____ him in time. (reached/reach)

6. We appreciate _____ us a sample. (you send/your sending)

7. We hope you will find our price _____. (agreeable/agreement)

8. Please be _____ that goods will reach you in time. (assured/ensured)

二、用所给词的正确形式填空

1. Your latest pattern is of _____ to us. (interest)

2. The importer and the exporter have reached an _____. (agree)

3. The seller requests a _____ irrevocable L/C. (confirm)

4. Please extend the insurance _____ to include All Risks. (cover)

5. Your early reply shall be much _____. (appreciate)

6. There is tough _____ in the overseas market. (compete)

7. Please keep us _____ of the details of insurance. (inform)

8. It's _____ that we cannot advance shipment as requested. (regret)

三、句子翻译

1. 请告知装运日期。

2. 很遗憾给贵公司带来诸多不便。

3. 货号为008的产品我们非常满意。

4. Your last shipment is of satisfaction to us and we decide to repeat an order.

5. While we appreciate the quality of your products, we feel your offer is not agreeable.

6. We believe it beneficial for you to reduce your price in consideration of keen competition in the market here.

三、普通英语VS专业术语

➤ 能力要求

掌握常见商函单词的专业术语含义。

➤ 知识储备

单词	普通英语含义	专业术语含义	含义强化
acceptance	接受	承兑	documents against **acceptance** （承兑交单）
average	平均数	平均 海损	fair **average** quality （良好平均品质） particular **average** （单独海损）
balance	平衡	剩余的钱、物	pay the **balance** （支付余额）
bear	熊；忍受	承担	**bear** the additional charges （承担额外费用）
book	书本	接受订货或预订 预定	**book** one's order （接受某人的订货） **book** shipping space （订舱）
capital	首都	资本	registered **capital** （注册资本）
can	能够	用罐头装	**canned** fruit （罐装水果）
clean	干净的	清洁的 光票	**clean** B/L （清洁提单） **clean** L/C （光票信用证）
copy	复印	份 副本	a **copy** of catalog （一份目录） original and **copy** （正本和副本）
collection	收集	托收	documentary **collection** （跟单托收）
confirm	确认	保兑	a **confirmed** L/C （保兑的信用证）
draw	绘画	向……开立	**draw** on sb. (a draft) （向某人开汇票）
deal	处理	交易	close a **deal** （成交）
duty	职责；值日	关税	import **duty** （进口关税）
end	末尾；终端	（通信方式相互联系之中的）一方	at our **end** （在本地）
fail	失败	未能（做到）	**fail** to supply goods （不能供货）

单词	普通英语含义	专业术语含义	含义强化
fair	公平的	交易会	trade **fair** （贸易会）
find	找到	觉得，认为	**find** sth. impossible （觉得某事不可能）
free	空闲的 免费的	免费的 无义务的， 责任免除的	**free** of charge （免费） **Free** Carrier （货交承运人）
general	总的	大体的，笼统的 公共的	a **general** idea of our goods （对我们产品的大概印象/大致了解） **general** average （共同海损）
handle	处理	经营 把手	**handle** shoes （经营鞋子） door **handle** （门把手）
honor	荣誉	接受	**honor** your draft （承兑你方汇票）
learn	学习	得知，获悉	**learn** your name from the Internet （从网络上获悉你方名号）
level	水平	行情	market **level** （市场行情）
line	线	经营范围	in the **line** of silk （在丝绸行业）
lot	许多	批次	shipment in three equal **lots** （分三批等量运输）
match	比赛	匹配	**match** the market level （与……市场行情一致）
nature	自然	本质，属性	goods of fragile **nature** （易碎性质的产品）
negotiation	谈判	磋商 议付	business **negotiation** （业务磋商） valid for **negotiation** in China （在中国议付有效）
offer	提供	提供，提供的事物 报盘	job **offer** （工作机会） a firm **offer** （实盘）
order	点菜，点单	订单，订购 秩序	a trial **order** （尝试性订单） in good **order** （状况良好）

单词	普通英语含义	专业术语含义	含义强化
party	晚会	一方,当事人	notify **party** （通知方）
place	地方	订货	**place** an order （下订单）
position	地方	处境	understand our **position** （理解我们的处境）
practice	练习	一贯的做法	usual **practice** （惯例）
present	礼物	递交	**present** the documents （交单）
right	正确的	权利	reserve the **right** to cancel the order （保留取消订单的权利）
share	分享	一份,份额	market **share** （市场份额）
sight	视力;看见	见票即付	**sight** draft （即期汇票）
stage	舞台	阶段	sales-pushing **stage** （促销阶段）
stand	站,立	展位,摊位	**stand** No.5 （5号摊位）
study	学习	参考,研究	for one's **study** （供某人研究）
subject	科目	标题 以……为准的	**subject** goods （标题货物） **subject** to our confirmation （以我们的确认为准）
term	学期	期限 术语	long-**term** cooperation （长期合作） price **term** （价格术语）
time	时间	远期	**time** L/C （远期信用证）
type	打字	类型,款式 典型	**Type** No. （型号） **type** sample （标准样品）
works	作品	工厂,车间	Ex **Works** （工厂外交货）
yard	院子	码	20 dollars per **yard** （每码20美元）

学习点拨

专业术语的特殊性要求我们注意平时积累、强化训练,才能有所收获。

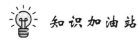 知识加油站

一词多义的英文单词如何理解记忆?

◎ 记住其中一个本义,利用**引申法**、**联想法**等展开记忆。

◎ 以大量阅读作为积累,在语境中利用**上下文**和**逻辑常识**进行合理推测。

◎ 注意经常使用,达到以练代记的目的。

注意:看似熟悉的单词也要仔细辨认,**避免望文生义**,如 banker(开户行)、means(方式,手段)、standing(资信)等。

巩固与提升

[真题在线]

短语或句子翻译

1. firm offer（2011年第81题）

2. 在中国议付有效（2011年第89题）

3. If you could order over 2,000 pieces of the offered item, we would allow a discount of 12%.（2011年第91题）

4. In most cases, our practice of payment is a confirmed, irrevocable sight L/C.（2012年第92题）

5. 交易磋商（2014年第77题）

6. voluntary offer（2015年第46题）

7. We would like to book with you a duplicate order for the same articles.（2015年第52题）

8. 共同海损（2018年第41题）

[强化练习] ··

一、词语互译

1. Delivered Duty Paid

2. time draft

3. in two equal lots

4. freight cost

5. 虚盘

6. 惯例

7. 标题货物

8. 市场份额

二、句子翻译

1. Your offer doesn't match the market level.

2. Both parties have reached an agreement in price.

3. Through the courtesy of ABC Company, we learn you're a leading exporter of garment.

4. If you can cut the price by 5%, we might come to terms.

5. 我们从2019年中国国际进口博览会获悉贵司的名号。

6. 为了弥补不断上涨的成本,我方不得不涨价5%。

7. 额外的保费由买家承担。

8. 我们对贵司228型号的产品颇感兴趣。

三、改错(找出句子中的一处错误并改正)

1. Payment by sight L/C is our usually practice.

2. Your products are of interest to us and we would like to place a trial order with 3,000 sets.

3. In view of our long-term cooperation, we decide to cut the price at 50 cents per piece.

4. Could you deliver the goods in three equally lots?

5. We have to adjust the price covering the growing cost.

6. This is our offer, subject at our final confirmation.

7. The insurance policy is usually issuing in duplicate.

8. The bank that confirms the L/C is called confirmed bank.

 ▶ 词缀篇

➤ **能力要求**

掌握名词、动词及形容词变化的常见词缀和特殊情形。

掌握常见的表示反义的词缀和特殊情形。

熟悉常见的前缀及其含义。

➤ **知识储备**

一、名词词缀

(一)常见的名词后缀

1. 动词变名词

(1)"-age"

breakage	carriage	coverage	leakage
package	pilferage	postage	storage

(2)"-ance"

accordance	allowance	assistance	assurance
compliance	conveyance	insurance	remittance

(3)"-ence"

dependence	existence	insistence	persistence

(4)"-er/-or"

dealer	exporter	insurer	underwriter
consignor	inspector	surveyor	supervisor

(5)"-ing"

beginning	cutting	feeling	loading
packing	sailing	standing	understanding

(6)"-ion/-tion/-ation"

attention	compensation	confirmation	destination
execution	hesitation	negotiation	quotation
reduction	reputation	stipulation	satisfaction

（7）"-ment"

arrangement	amendment	commitment	consignment
establishment	reimbursement	requirement	settlement

2. 形容词变名词

（1）"-ence"

absence	confidence	difference	excellence
inconvenience	independence	patience	presence

（2）"-ity"

activity	equality	productivity	popularity
priority	reality	superiority	validity

（3）"-ancy/-ency"

currency	discrepancy	emergency	urgency

（4）"-ness"

carelessness	competitiveness	exactness	kindness

（5）"-ht/-th"

height	length	strength	width

（二）特殊的名词后缀

1. 以"-al"结尾的名词（动词变名词）

arrival	approval	disposal	perusal
proposal	refusal	removal	withdrawal

2. 以"-y"结尾的名词（动词通常以-er/-re结尾）

delivery	enquiry	entry	expiry

3. 以"-plicate"结尾表示一式几份

duplicate	triplicate	quadruplicate	quintuplicate

4. 以"-ship"结尾表示性质、状况、身份等

friendship	ownership	relationship	workmanship

5. 以"-ure"结尾表示状态、行为,以及行为的结果、情况等

departure	enclosure	failure	pleasure

6. "-er/-ee""-or/-ee"一组出现表示对等关系

addresser/addressee	drawer/drawee
transferor/transferee	consignor/consignee

7. "-ware"表示物体总称

hardware	kitchenware	software	tableware

二、动词词缀

1. "en-/-en"表示"使……变成"

enable	encourage	enclose	ensure

| broaden | hasten | shorten | widen |

2. "-fy/-ify"表示"……化,加强"

| classify | clarify | identify | modify |
| qualify | notify | simplify | specify |

3. "-ize"表示"……化"

| apologize | industrialize | minimize | organize |
| particularize | popularize | realize | specialize |

4. "be-"表示"使,使成为……"

| become | behave | beware |

三、形容词词缀

1. 常见的形容词词缀

（1）"-able"

| agreeable | available | coverable | irrevocable |
| payable | profitable | reliable | salable |

（2）"-ful"

| careful | faithful | grateful | hopeful |
| regretful | skillful | thankful | useful |

（3）"-al/-ial/-ual"

actual	additional	beneficial	commercial
continual	financial	global	initial
international	optional	potential	punctual

（4）"-ive"

| active | attractive | effective | excessive |
| exclusive | inclusive | prospective | relative |

（5）"-ant/-ent"

| assistant | reluctant | pleasant | relevant |
| different | excellent | present | subsequent |

（6）"-ous"

| continuous | desirous | famous | various |

（7）"-some"

| awesome | handsome | troublesome |

（8）"-y"

| faulty | risky | rusty | stormy |

2. 特殊的形容词词缀

（1）"-ary"表示"有……性质的,属于……的,关于……的"

| customary | documentary | monetary | voluntary |

（2）"-en"表示"由……制成的,有……质"

| golden | silken | wooden | woolen |

（3）"-ior"表示"较……的"

| inferior | prior | senior | superior |

四、反义词缀

1. 常见的反义词词缀

（1）"dis-"

| disagree | dishonor | dislike | dissatisfaction |

（2）"im-"

| impatient | imperfect | impolite | impossible |

（3）"-less"

| careless | hopeless | regardless | useless |

（4）"mis-"

| misfortune | mislead | mis-sent | misunderstand |

（5）"un-"

| unclear | unfortunately | unlikely | unpopular |

2. 特殊的反义词词缀

（1）"counter-"

| countersign | counter-offer | counteract | counterpart |

（2）"de-"

| degrade | decode | depreciate | devaluation |

（3）"in-"

| inability | inaccurate | inadequate | incomplete |
| inconvenience | incorrect | insufficient | invisible |

（4）"il-"

| illegal | illimitable | illogical |

（5）"ir-"

| irrevocable | irregular | irrespective | irrelevant |

（6）"non-"

| non-delivery | non-firm | non-negotiable | nonstop |

五、其他常见前缀

1. "a-"用来加强含义,如 alike, amend, await。

2. "a-"表示"在……的",如 aside, ahead, around。

3. "ab-"表示"相反",如 absent, abuse, abnormal。

4. "be-"表示"在",如 beside, behind, below。

5. "co-"表示"合、一起"，如 cooperate，correspond，coordination。

6. "com-"表示"共同"，如 combine，company，compare。

7. "e-/ex-"表示"(位置、方向)向外"，如 export，exclude。

8. "fore-"表示"前部，提前"，如 forecast，foresee。

9. "inter-"表示"在之间，相互"，如 international，interchange，interview。

10. "mini-"表示"小，迷你"，如 minimum，minimize，miniskirt。

11. "over-"表示"过度，过分"，如 overdue，overestimated。

12. "pre-"表示"前，先"，如 prepaid，previous。

13. "re-"表示"又、再"，如 reconsider，refund。

14. "tele-"表示"电"，如 telephone，telex，telegraphic。

15. "trans-"表示"越过，跨过"，如 transport，transship。

16. "under-"表示"下面的"，如 underground，under-mentioned。

 学习点拨

作为非独立个体，词缀需要依附其他单词存在。按照其在单词中所处的位置，词缀可以分为**前缀和后缀两类**。

词缀一般有自己的含义，有的可能还不止一种含义。它同词干组合构成新的单词，在推测时必须充分把握其词义及词性。

 知识加油站

以"-ly"结尾的形容词

◎ 名词加"-ly"，表示"具备……特征的"：

friendly(友好的)   lovely(可爱的)

◎ 表示时间的词加"-ly"，表示"每……的"：

daily(每日的)   weekly(每周的)

monthly(每月的)   quarterly(每个季度的)

◎ 特殊情况：

costly(昂贵的)   deadly(致命的)

likely(很有可能的)   timely(及时的)

巩固与提升

[真题在线]

一、单项选择题

Please send us your confirmation of sales in _____.（2013年第64题）

A. two copy   B. two pieces   C. twice   D. duplicate

二、短语或句子翻译

1. L/C amendment（2011年第83题）

2. The insurance is to be covered by sellers for 110% of invoice value against Clash and Breakage Risk in addition to W. P. A.（2011年第94题）

3. We hope you will establish the relative L/C before the end of this month.（2012年第91题）

4. financial status（2018年第44题）

5. drawee bank（2019年第48题）

[强化练习]

一、根据要求进行词性变化

1. 将下列动词变成其相应名词

① extend   ② enquire   ③ require   ④ propose

⑤ convey   ⑥ break   ⑦ pack   ⑧ satisfy

2. 将下列词变成其反义词

① regard   ② revocable   ③ agreement   ④ understanding

⑤ stable   ⑥ transferable   ⑦ regular   ⑧ capable

二、用所给词的正确形式填空

1. Please note the _____ of L/C is till June 28.（valid）

2. We regret that your offer is too high to be _____.（accept）

3. We're sorry for the _____ caused.（convenient）

4. The seller made a sincere _____ to its partner.（apologize）

5. We regret our _____ to deliver the goods as scheduled.（able）

6. They have _____ the client of the shipping date. (information)

7. We have decided to allow you a special discount, eyeing for the _____ of sales. (promote)

8. We shall appreciate it if you give _____ to our proposal. (prior)

三、句子翻译

1. We anticipate your early confirmation of our order.

2. The under-mentioned goods are available from stock.

3. Please note our minimum order is 5,000 yards.

4. It is impossible for us to accept your order at present owing to heavy commitment.

5. Please reconsider our revised price and expect your approval at your earliest convenience.

6. In international trade, the conclusion of a business usually goes through many rounds of negotiation.

7. Two parties reached an agreement finally and the contract came into force.

8. Please make delivery of the goods within the time stipulated to enable us to catch the selling season.

 词组篇

一、同义、近义词汇总

➤ **能力要求**

掌握函电考试中同一中文词汇的不同英文表述。

➤ **知识储备**

1. 公司

| company | Co., Ltd | corporation | firm |

2. 产品,货物

article	consignment	cargo	item
freight	goods	merchandise	produce
product	shipment		

3. 地区,区域

| area | district | region |

4. 经营

| handle | deal in | specialize in | be in the line of |

5. 同某人建交

enter into/establish business relations with sb.

build up relationship with sb.

open an account with sb.

6. 和,一起

| as well as | together with | in addition to |

7. 另邮,另寄

| under separate cover | by separate post/mail |

8. 畅销

| sell fast/well | be popular/salable | enjoy great popularity |
| command a good market | be widely accepted | |

9. 资信,信用

| status | standing | credit | reputation |

10. 因某事向某人感谢

be obliged/grateful/thankful for sth. to sb.

11. 向某人报价

make sb. an offer for sth.

quote/offer sb. the price for sth.

send sb the quotation/offer

12. 减价,降价

cut/reduce/lower the price（by/to...）   make a reduction（of...）

13. 涨价

（sb.）raise/increase the price   （price）go up/increase/rise

14. 给某人折扣

allow/offer/give/grant sb. a discount

15. 要求,需求

demand   need   requirement   request

16. 有潜力（市场）

promising   potential   prospective

17. 成交

come to terms   reach an agreement

conclude the transaction   close a deal

18. 通知、告知

notify/inform/advise sb. of sth.

19. 可供现货

be shipped/supplied/available from stock

20. 发送某物

send/deliver/dispatch/ship/transport/forward sth.

21. 剩余的（货）

the rest   the balance   the remainder   the remaining

22. 办理保险

make/effect/cover/take out insurance

23. 开立信用证

open/establish/issue an L/C

24. 惯例

usual/general/customary practice

25. 费用

cost   expense   fee   charge

26. 由······付款

at one's expense/for one's account/be borne by sb.

27.（条款、价格等）与······一致

be in accordance with   be in line with agree with/be in agreement with

conform to/be in conformity to

comply with/be in compliance with

be consistent with

28. 关于,有关

about/on　　　　　　　　　as for/as to　　　　　　concerning/covering

regarding/with regard to/as regards　　　　　　referring to/with reference to

29. 相关的,有关的

relevant/relative/covering(放在名词前居多)

concerned(放在名词后居多)

related(放在名词前、后皆可)

30. 为了(表目的)

for + sth.

so as to/in order to/to + do sth.

with a view to + doing sth.

31. 建议(某人)做某事

advise to do sth./advise sb. to do sth.

propose to do sth.

suggest doing sth./suggest sb's doing sth.

32. 期待(某人)做某事

hope to do sth./hope that...

expect to do sth./expect sb. to do sth./expect that...

anticipate doing sth./anticipate sb.'s doing sth.

look forward to doing sth./look forward to sb's doing sth.

long for sth./doing sth.

33. 尽力做某事

try one's best /do one's utmost /make every effort to do sth.

34. 向某人提出索赔

lodge/file/raise a claim against sb.

35. 条款

provision　　　　　　　stipulation　　　　　clause　　　　　　terms

36. 合同,合约

sales contract　　　　purchase contract　　　sales confirmation　　purchase order

37. (向某人)提供(某物)

provide sb. with sth./provide sth. for sb.

supply sb. with sth./supply sth. to sb.

offer sb. sth./offer sth. to sb.

furnish sb. with sth.

38. 充分利用

make full use of　　　　make the best of　　　take full advantage of

39. 考虑到,鉴于

considering　　　　　in consideration of　　in view of

40. 装运日期

date of shipment   shipping date   shipment date

41. 装船通知

shipping advice   declaration of shipment   notice of shipment

42. 别无他法,只得……

can do nothing but do sth.

have nothing to do but do sth.

have no choice/alternative but to do sth.

43. 联系(某人)

get in touch with sb.   contact sb.   approach sb.

44. 在这种情况下

such being the case   in this case   under the circumstances

 学习点拨

同一个中文含义使用不同的英文表述,增加了考试的难度,特别是在中翻英和商函写作部分。除了强化记忆以外,可以使用**思维导图**来进行归纳和记忆。平时训练时,**有意识地使用新学习的词汇来表述**,为日后的使用奠定基础。

 知识加油站

同义词在使用时的注意点

◎ 同一个中文含义可以使用不同的英文表述,但这些英文也存在一些轻微区别。如"货物"一词,produce 一般指"土特产",consignment 指"寄售的货物",而 goods 一般指"工业制成品"。

◎ 同一个中文含义可以使用不同的英文表述,这些英文可能在使用中存在差异。如"关系"一词,relation 是可数名词,而 relationship 则是不可数名词。

◎ 表示同一个含义的动词,搭配的宾语也会有差异。如"建议"一词,propose 后接 to do sth.,而suggest 后接 doing sth.。

巩固与提升

[真题在线]

一、句子翻译

1. We are very interested in your goods, so _____

_____(请报给我方600吨下列货物的最低价). (2012年第86题)

2. We will place a trial order with you, _____
_____. （假如你方可以给我方5%的折扣）（2013年第86题）

3. We would be grateful _____ .
（如果你方能尽快发货）（2013年第87题）

4. We regret to say that _____（我们不可能
再降价了）as there is little profit for such goods now.（2014年第89题）

5. 如果每个款式的购买不少于1000码的话，我们可给2%的折扣。（2016年第56题）

6. 我们借此机会与贵方建立业务关系。（2018年第56题）

［强化练习］

一、单项选择题

1. The samples will be sent _____ separate cover.

   A. at   B. in   C. under   D. by

2. The terms in L/C should _____ those in the contract.

   A. comply to   B. conform to   C. agree on   D. confirm to

3. _____, we are making you the following offer.

   A. As your request   B. As requested

   C. At your requested   D. At you request

4. The company, _____ in 1985, is a leading one in the line of silk scarf.

   A. established   B. establishing   C. establishment   D. was established

5. Such being the case, we _____ but to raise the price _____ 5%.

   A. can do nothing; to   B. can do nothing; by

   C. have no choice; to   D. have no choice; by

6. To avoid unnecessary trouble, would you please have the L/C _____ in the contracted time?

   A. issue   B. issuing   C. issued   D. to issue

7. Your claim on the shortage of weight should be _____ with the insurance company.

   A. met   B. filed   C. given   D. rose

8. The good opportunity should _____.

   A. make use   B. make use of

   C. be made use   D. be made use of

二、用所给词的正确形式填空

1. To develop the market, we intend _____ you a special discount.（allow）

2. We anticipate with pleasure _____ your favorable reply.（receive）

3. With a view to _____ our first deal, we decide to cut the price to $ 5/yard.（close）

4. The seller proposed that payment _____ by sight L/C.（make）

5. It is our customary practice _____ business on sight L/C basis.（do）

6. We will do everything we can _____ your requirements.（satisfy）

7. We are glad to inform you that the goods enjoy great _____. (popular)

8. _____ to S/C 123, would you please expedite shipment?(refer)

三、句子翻译

1. 请确保信用证条款与合同条款完全一致。

2. 能否提供一些样品供我们参考?

3. 不用说,额外的保费将由我们支付。

4. 第一批货物在6月份交,其余的在7月份交。

5. 经营家电30多年,我们同国内外的客户建立了良好的关系。

6. 请尽力开来信用证以便于我们早日交货。

7. 目录连同最新的价目表将另邮。

二、外贸商函术语大分类

➤ 能力要求

掌握同一术语的不同分类的表述。

➤ 知识储备

1. 企业

private enterprise	state-owned company	medium-sized corporation
私营企业	国有企业	中型企业

2. 目录

latest catalogue	complete catalogue	illustrated catalogue
最新目录	完整目录	图解目录

3. 样品

duplicate sample	counter sample	reference sample
复样	对等样品	参考样品
keep sample	seal sample	shipping sample
留样	封样	船样

4. 价格

unit price	retail price	wholesale price
单价	零售价	批发价

competitive price	realistic price	workable price
有竞争力的价格	符合实际的价格	可行的价格

5. 关系

cooperative relations	long-term relations	mutually beneficial relations
合作关系	长期关系	互利的关系

6. 报盘

a firm offer	a non-firm offer	a voluntary offer
实盘	虚盘	主动报盘

7. 折扣

quantity discount	trade discount	special discount
数量折扣	贸易折扣	特殊折扣

8. 订单

fresh order	trial order	sample order
新订单	试订单	样品单
duplicate order	repeat/repeated order	
复订单	续订单	

9. 成本,费用

labor cost	production cost	freight cost
劳动力成本	生产成本	运费成本
purchase cost	banking charges	additional charges
采购成本	银行费用	额外的费用

10. 船

steamer	vessel	tramp
船只	船只	不定期船
liner	direct steamer	container ship
班轮	直达船	集装箱船

11. 港口

port of loading	port of destination	port of unloading
装运港	目的港	卸货港
port of discharge	port of transshipment	optional port
卸货港	转运港	选择港

12. 集装箱

air-tight container	dry container	container yard
密封集装箱	干货集装箱	集装箱堆场
container freight station	full container load	less than container load
集装箱货运站	整箱货	拼箱货

13. 提单

order B/L	straight B/L	blank B/L
指示提单	记名提单	不记名提单

through B/L	clean B/L	foul B/L
联运提单	清洁提单	不清洁提单

14. 银行

(1)汇付方式

remitting bank	paying/receiving bank
汇出行	汇入行

(2)托收方式

remitting bank	collecting bank	presenting bank
托收行	代收行	提示行

(3)信用证方式

opening/issuing bank	advising/notifying bank	paying/drawee bank
开证行	通知行	付款行
negotiating bank	confirming bank	accepting bank
议付行	保兑行	承兑行
reimbursing bank		
偿付行		

15. 信用证

confirmed L/C	irrevocable L/C	documentary L/C
保兑的信用证	不可撤销信用证	跟单信用证
clean L/C	sight L/C	time/usance L/C
光票信用证	即期信用证	远期信用证
revolving L/C	back-to-back credit	reciprocal credit
循环信用证	对背信用证	对开信用证

16. 发票

commercial invoice	proforma invoice	customs invoice
商业发票	形式发票	海关发票
consular invoice	receipt invoice	
领事发票	钱货两讫发票/收妥发票	

17. 保单

insurance application	insurance policy	insurance certificate
投保单	保险单	保险凭证
open policy	cover note	
预约保单	暂保单	

18. 损失

total loss	partial loss	actual loss
全损	部分损失	实际损失
general average	particular average	constructive total loss
共同海损	单独海损	推定全损

三、外贸商函专业术语大集合

➤ **能力要求**

熟悉常见的外贸术语的专业含义。

掌握常见的外贸术语的英文表述。

➤ **知识储备**

(一)货物篇(Goods)

1. 品名 name of commodity

2. 商标 trade mark

3. 规格 specifications

4. 等级 grade

5. 标准 standard

6. 品质公差 quality tolerance

7. 吨 metric ton

8. 长吨 long ton

9. 短吨 short ton

10. 毛重 gross weight

11. 净重 net weight

12. 溢短装条款 more or less clause

13. 运输标志 shipping marks

14. 警告标志 warning marks

15. 中性包装 neutral packing

16. 内包装 inner packing

17. 外包装 outer packing

18. 适合海运包装 seaworthy packing

19. 散货 bulk cargo

(二)贸易术语篇(Trade Term)

1. 贸易术语 trade term

2. 条件 terms and conditions

3. 货币 currency

4. 净价 net price

5. 询价单 enquiry sheet

6. 报价单 quotation sheet

7. 折扣 discount/allowance

8. 佣金 commission

9. 询盘 enquiry/inquiry

10. 报盘 offer

11. 还盘 counter-offer

12. 接受 acceptance

13. 象征性交货 symbolic delivery

14. 终点站交货 Delivered at Terminal（DAT）

15. 目的地交货 Delivered at Place（DAP）

16. 完税后交货 Delivered Duty Paid（DDP）

（三）运输篇（Transportation）

1. 承运人 carrier

2. 货代 freight forwarder/forwarding agent

3. 运费 freight/carriage

4. 运费待付 freight to collect

5. 运费预付 freight prepaid

6. 空舱费 dead freight

7. 滞期费 demurrage

8. 速遣费 dispatch money/despatch

9. 定程租船 voyage charter

10. 定期租船 time charter

11. 装船指示 shipping instructions

12. 重量/尺码吨 weight/measurement ton

13. 多式运输 multimodal transport/combined transport

14. 大副收据 mate's receipt

15. 装货单/关单 shipping order

16. 场站收据 Dock Receipt（D/R）

17. 装货清单 Loading List（L/T）

18. 货损通知书 notice of claim

19. 预计到达时间 Estimated Time of Arrival（ETA）

20. 预计离港时间 Estimated Time of Departure（ETD）

（四）保险篇（Insurance）

1. 发票金额 invoice value

2. 保险金额 insurance amount

3. 保险费率 insurance rate

4. 保费 premium

5. 险别 coverage

6. 保险人 insurer

7. 被保险人 the insured

8. 承保人 underwriter

9. 一般附加险 general additional risk

10. 特殊附加险 special additional risk

11. 免赔额 franchise

12. 仓至仓条款 warehouse to warehouse clause

(五)支付篇(Payment)

1. 外汇 foreign exchange

2. 汇率 exchange rate

3. 汇付 remittance

4. 托收 collection

5. 电汇 telegraphic transfer

6. 信汇 mail transfer

7. 票汇 demand draft

8. 汇票 draft/bill of exchange

9. 远期汇票 time/usance draft

10. 支付工具 instruments of payment

11. 本票 promissory note

12. 银行保函 banker's Letter of Guarantee(L/G)

13. 预付货款 payment in advance

14. 货到付款 payment after arrival of the goods

15. 凭单付现 cash against documents

16. 分期付款 payment by installments

17. 赊销 Open Account(O/A)

18. 提示 presentation

19. 拒付 dishonor

20. 光票 clean bill

21. 空白背书 blank endorsement

(六)检验、索赔、不可抗力和仲裁(Inspection，Claim，Force Majeure & Arbitration)

1. 品质检验证书 inspection certificate of quality

2. 产地检验证书 inspection certificate of origin

3. 数量检验证书 inspection certificate of quantity

4. 重量检验证书 inspection certificate of weight

5. 检验报告 survey report

6. 检验证书 survey certificate

7. 品质不良 inferior quality

8. 短交 short delivery

9. 争议 dispute

10. 投诉 complaint

11. 异议与索赔 discrepancy and claim

12. 罚金 penalty

13. 不可抗力 force majeure

14. 仲裁 arbitration

（七）其他（Others）

1. 海关发票 customs invoice

2. 关税 duty/tariff

3. 进口/出口许可证 import/export license

4. 独家代理 exclusive/sole agency

5. 寄售 consignment

6. 补偿贸易 compensation trade

7. 出口退税 export tax rebate

8. 电子商务 e-commerce

 学习点拨

专业词汇具有其特殊性，书写时，要注意细节，特别是一些外来词汇，如不可抗力（force majeure）、形式发票（proforma invoice）等。使用时，不可望文生义，如标准样品应是 type sample，而不是 standard sample。

 知识加油站

源自中文（音译）的商品词汇

bonsai 盆栽	cheongsam 旗袍	dim sum 点心
ginseng 人参	longan 龙眼	lychee 荔枝
oolong 乌龙（茶）	silk 丝绸	typhoon 台风

巩固与提升

[真题在线]

词语互译

1. 电汇（2011年第75题）

2. 装运通知（2012年第75题）

3. 形式发票（2012年第78题）

4. 保险费（2013年第76题）

5. 收货人（2014年第78题）　　　　　6. declaration of shipment（2015年第48题）

7. 对开信用证（2016年第41题）　　　　8. 重复订单（2016年第42题）

9. delivery against letter of guarantee（2017年第45题）

[强化练习] ··

一、词语互译

1. 标准样品　　　　　　　　　　　　2. 以毛作净

3. 通知方　　　　　　　　　　　　　4. 具体询盘

5. 集装箱堆场　　　　　　　　　　　6. 最低起订量

7. force majeure　　　　　　　　　　8. registered capital

9. weight memo　　　　　　　　　　10. merchant vessel

11. customs invoice　　　　　　　　12. export license

二、句子翻译

1. We will remit you the full value by T/T.

2. The risk is coverable at a rate of 0.7%.

3. In the event of loss or damage, you should contact the underwriter without delay.

4. The continual rise in various costs forced the manufacturer to adjust the price accordingly.

5. The exporter desires payment in advance while the importer prefers open account.

6. The loss, due to your improper packing, totals 2,500 dollars.

7. Quantity: 30,000 yards, with 5% more or less at seller's option.

8. In case of dispute in quality, survey report must be presented as evidence.

常用句子篇

➤ **能力要求**

熟悉在外贸主要环节中使用的重点句子。
掌握常见的重点句子的含义。

➤ **知识储备**

一、建立业务关系

1. 获取客户信息的渠道

(1)We learned your name and e-mail address from the Internet.

我们从网络获悉贵司名号及邮件地址。

(2)We owe your name to our trade partner.

我们从贸易伙伴处获悉贵司名号。

(3)We have obtained your name and address from China International Import Expo.

我们从中国国际进口博览会获悉贵司名号及地址。

(4)On the recommendation of..., we learn you are a leading exporter of...

在××的推荐下,我们获悉你们是××产品的大出口商。

(5)Through the courtesy of ABC Co. in your region, we understand that you import/export...

通过贵地ABC公司的介绍,我们了解到贵司进口/出口……

2. 期待建立业务关系

(1)We anticipate the pleasure of entering into business relationship.

我们企盼着建立业务关系。

(2)Looking forward to establishment of business relations on the basis of mutual benefit.

期待在互利的基础上建立业务关系。

(3)We are desirous of establishing mutually beneficial business relations.

渴望同贵司建立互利的业务关系。

(4)We are writing in the hope of opening an account with your company.

现致函,期待同贵司建立业务关系。

(5)Your wish to initiate business relationship coincides with us.

你方想同我方建立业务关系的想法与我方不谋而合。

3. 公司介绍

(1) Established in 1980, we export garments of high quality.

本公司创立于1980年,出口高品质的服装。

(2) Our main business is importing red wine.

我们的主营业务是进口红酒。

(3) We are an importer of farm produce with a registered capital of 2 million dollars.

我们是一家农产品进口公司,注册资本200万美元。

(4) We, a Shanghai-based company, specialize in the export of silk with many years' experience.

本公司位于上海,专营丝绸出口业务,有多年的经验。

(5) We have been in the line for over 20 years and have wide connections with clients all over the world.

我们经营该业务有20多年了,与世界各地的客户有广泛的联系。

4. 产品介绍

(1) Our goods are of nice colors, novel designs and good workmanship.

我们的产品颜色鲜艳、设计新颖、工艺精湛。

(2) Our goods, made of premium raw material, enjoy high quality.

我们的产品由优质原料制成,品质优良。

(3) Our products command a good market in East China.

我们的产品在华东地区畅销。

(4) These are our latest goods, which are salable in overseas market.

这是我们的新产品,在海外市场畅销。

(5) Compared with those from neighboring countries, ours are of better quality.

与邻国产品相比,我们产品的品质略胜一筹。

5. 寄送产品资料及样品

(1) Enclosed please find a copy of our e-catalog.

随函附寄电子目录一份,请查收。

(2) Attached is the brochure needed.

附寄一份贵司需要的小册子。

(3) To let you have a general idea of our goods, we're now sending you a catalog for your perusal.

为了使你们对我们的产品有一个大概印象,现寄一份目录供详阅。

(4) Samples will be forwarded by separate mail.

样品另邮。

(5) Samples are free of charge, but postage is for your account.

样品免费,但贵司要承担邮费。

6. 向银行或其他渠道调查客户资信

(1) We should be most grateful for any information you may provide concerning ABC Co.

我们会非常感谢您提供有关ABC公司的任何信息。

(2) Would you be kind enough to offer us information covering the standing of the above firm?

能否提供上述公司的资信信息给我们?

(3) You are given as a reference by ABC Company.

ABC公司把贵司作为(资信)推荐人/参考人。

(4)Any information you may provide will be treated in strict confidence.

你方提供的任何信息都将严格保密。

7. 结尾语句

(1)Expecting favorable reply at your earliest convenience.

希望贵司尽早给予答复。

(2)Anticipating our profitable business in the near future.

期盼双方未来的业务会让彼此收益颇丰。

(3)We hope to hear from you soon.

盼早复。

(4)We await your early response with keen interest.

殷切期待贵司早复。

二、询盘和报盘

1. 向客户询盘

(1)Your goods Item No.02 are of interest to us. Would you please let us know your lowest price?

我们对货号02的产品感兴趣。能否告知最低价？

(2)Could you offer us your most favorable CFR London price?

能否报CFR伦敦最优价？

(3)Could you quote us on CIF Amsterdam basis for Golden Star TV?

能否就金星电视机向我们报CIF阿姆斯特丹价？

(4)Please inform us of your minimum order.

请告知你们的最低起订量。

2. 报价及有效期

(1)As requested, we're now making you the following offer, based on an order not less than 5,000 pieces.

按要求,现就订单不少于5000件向你们报价如下。

(2)In reply to your enquiry dated May 5th, we are now quoting as follows.

兹回复贵司5月5日来函,现报价如下。

(3)We are sending you our offer today, which is firm in May only.

现向你报价,该报价只在5月有效。

(4)Please note our offer keeps open for 7 days only.

请注意我们报价的有效期只有7天。

(5)This is our offer for goods Item No. 08, which remains valid till June 15th.

这是我们对货号为08的产品的报价,该报价一直保持到6月15日有效。

三、还盘和反还盘

1. 阐述不能接受报价

（1）Much to our regret, your price is on the high side.

很遗憾,你方价格偏高。

（2）We regret our inability to accept your offer for garment Article No.02.

很遗憾,我方不能接受你方对货号02服装的报价。

（3）It is regrettable that your price is out of line with the prevailing market level.

很遗憾,你方价格与现行市场价格不一致。

（4）We find your quotation doesn't match the market level here.

我们觉得你方价格与本地市场不匹配。

（5）We have to point out with regret that your offer cannot compete with those from other sources.

很遗憾,我们不得不指出你们的报价不能同其他渠道的报价相竞争。

2. 要求对方降价

（1）We expect you to reduce the price by 5%.

期待你方降价5%。

（2）Would it be possible to cut your price to \$25 per piece?

能否降价到25美元一件?

（3）We wonder if there is any room for price reduction.

我们想知道是否有降价空间。

（4）Your price is so high that we have to turn to other manufacturers.

你方价格太高,我们只得向其他厂家订货。

3. 拒绝对方降价请求

（1）We are unable to comply with your request for a reduction of 5%.

你方要求降价5%,我们不能满足。

（2）Our quotation is based on various costs and only includes small profit.

我们的报价建立在各种成本基础之上,所含利润微薄。

（3）Our original price leaves us with narrow margin of profit.

我们原来的报价使我们获利甚微。

（4）To be frank, quite a few orders have rushed in recently.

坦诚地说,近期大量订单蜂拥而至。

（5）We can do nothing but reject your request.

我们别无他法只得拒绝你方的要求。

4. 同对方就价格进行再次协商

（1）Much as we would like to meet your request, we find your counter-offer unacceptable.

尽管我们很想满足你方要求,但我们觉得你方还盘不能接受。

（2）Our price may be slightly higher, but our quality justifies it.

我方价格也许略高,但我们的品质证明价格是合理的。

（3）As a matter of fact，our price has been widely accepted in EU countries.

事实上，我们的价格在欧盟各国被广泛接受。

（4）To develop sales at your end，we are prepared to meet you half way.

为了推动产品在贵地的销售，我们愿意各让一半。

（5）The maximum concession is a reduction of 5%.

最大让步就是减价5%。

5. 满足客户低价格成交的对策

（1）If you place an order for 5,000 yards，we can lower the price.

若订购5000码，我们可以降价。

（2）In case your order arrives at us this month，your request for price reduction can be met.

若订单本月到达我方，我们可以满足你方的降价要求。

（3）We recommend goods Art. No. 01 as an excellent substitute at the price you demanded.

按照你方要求的价格，我们推荐货号为01的货物作为极佳的替代品。

（4）Product Item No. 02 is of similar function to the product demanded at a lower price.

02号产品的功能与你方需求的产品相似，且价格较低。

（5）If you insist on the original price，we advise you to replace what you need by a similar product.

若你方坚持原价，我们建议你方用类似的产品代替你方所需的产品。

6. 告知对方货物涨价

（1）We regret we have to raise the price by 5%. The new price takes effect from Oct. 1st.

很遗憾，我们不得不涨价5%。新价格从10月1日开始生效。

（2）As a result of the rising cost，we have to increase the price accordingly.

由于成本一直上涨，我们不得不相应涨价。

（3）The costs have increased sharply in the past few months. We have no alternative but to increase the selling price.

过去几个月成本上猛涨。我们别无选择只得提高销售价格。

（4）Much as we would like to keep our previous price，the rise in raw material made it impossible.

我们也很想保持原先的价格，但原材料价格的上涨使得这不可能。

（5）The rise in the price，mainly resulting from freight cost，forces us to adjust the price.

价格上涨的主要因素是运费成本，迫使我们调价。

四、成交与续购

1. 双方达成交易

（1）We would like to place an order for 10 tons of canned fruits at the agreed price.

我们想按双方商定的价格订购10吨罐头水果。

（2）Both parties have agreed on the terms and closed the deal.

双方已就条款达成一致并完成了交易。

（3）We confirm your order No. AH01 for 800 sets of Golden Deer Color TVs.

我们确认你方订购800台金鹿彩电的AH01订单。

（4）We agree to sell the following goods on terms and conditions below.

我们同意按下列条款和条件出售下列货物。

2. 续购

（1）Your goods are quite satisfactory and we hope to repeat an order.

我们对你方产品很满意，希望续订。

（2）Goods per S.S "Sailor" turn out to our entire satisfaction and we need another 5,000 sets.

装载在"水手"号上的货物让我们非常满意，我们要再购买5000套。

（3）We're in urgent need of additional quantities to complete our deliveries to our customers and wish to book a repeat order for 3,000 cartons.

我们急需追加产品数量向客户交货，希望续订3000箱。

（4）We desire extra quantities as a result of inadequate stock.

由于库存不足，我们想追加订购量。

（5）It is selling season and we need adequate stock to meet customers' needs.

现在是销售旺季，我们需要充足的库存满足客户需求。

3. 告知客户无货及对策

（1）We are sorry that the goods needed are out of stock currently.

很抱歉，你们需要的货物目前缺货。

（2）We regret the goods you ordered cannot be supplied from stock for the time being.

很遗憾，你们订购的货物暂时不能供货。

（3）We're fully committed and are not in a position to meet your request for extra quantity.

我们履约过多，不能满足你们额外数量的要求。

（4）We'll contact you as soon as our new supplies come in.

新货一到，我们立刻联系你方。

（5）We have products of similar function. Please let us know if you're interested.

我们有相似功能的产品。如有兴趣，敬请告知。

五、保　险

1. 请求对方代办保险

（1）Could you cover insurance on our behalf?

能代我们办理保险吗？

（2）Could you take out insurance for our account this time?

这次能否替我们投保？

（3）We think it convenient to have the goods insured at your end.

我们认为在贵地投保比较方便。

（4）We need your assistance in the field of insurance.

我们需要你方在保险上予以支持。

2. 请求扩大保险范围

（1）Would you please extend insurance coverage to include Clash and Breakage Risks?

能否扩大保险范围包括碰损破碎险？

（2）Since the goods are liable to be spoiled, we request you to cover additional risks.

由于货物易损坏，我们要求你方投保附加险。

（3）FPA is not good enough as our goods are delicate.

由于货物易损，平安险不够。

（4）WPA is too narrow for the goods of this nature. We require a broader coverage.

对于这种属性的货物而言，水渍险保障范围不够。我们需要保障范围更广的保险。

（5）We need a wider coverage for the goods and the extra premium is of course borne by us.

我们需要为货物投保更多险种。当然，额外的保费由我们承担。

3. 邮寄保单及索取额外保费

（1）The insurance policy will be forwarded to you soon once it is issued.

保单一旦签发，立刻寄送给您。

（2）We are enclosing the insurance policy and debit note for the premium.

随函附上保险单和保险费的借记单。

（3）Your request for broader coverage can be satisfied.

你们要求更多保险，我们可以满足。

（4）The additional risk has been covered and the extra premium is for your account.

追加的保险可以投保，额外保费由你们支付。

（5）We have covered the extra insurance required and shall appreciate your refunding the premium at an early date.

我们已投保了所需的额外保险。如能早日退还保险费，将不胜感激。

六、运 输

1. 催促发货

（1）We haven't received any information about shipment. Would you please expedite shipment?

我们未收到装运的任何消息。能否加快发货？

（2）As scheduled, the goods should have been shipped on Monday, but there is no information on shipment till today.

按计划，货物本应在星期一装船，但时至今日仍没有装船的消息。

（3）Punctual shipment is of great importance and we expect your timely delivery.

准时发货很重要，我们希望你方能及时交货。

（4）We're in urgent of the goods under Order No. 098 as our clients have pressed us twice.

我方急需098号订单项下的货物，因为我方客户已催促我方两次了。

（5）Your failure to deliver the goods in time will definitely cause us much inconvenience and it is also no good for you at the same time.

你方未能及时交货肯定会给我们带来许多不便，同时这也对你方不利。

2. 落实发货

（1）We have booked shipping space long before. There is no need to worry about it.

我们早就订好了舱位,贵司不用担心。

（2）We have pressed the factory and all the goods will be ready as scheduled. We assure you that they will reach you in due course.

我们已经催促工厂,所有的货物都将如期备好。我们向你保证它们会准时到达。

（3）The goods are ready for shipment and will be sent next Monday.

货物已经备妥,下周一出运。

（4）We're pleased to inform you that the goods have been shipped per S.S. "Victory" and are due to reach you as promised.

兹欣告货物已经装在"胜利号"上,它们会按先前的约定/承诺到达你处。

（5）We have shipped goods on board S.S. "Red Sea" and hope they will reach you in good order.

我们已将货物装在"红海"轮上,希望它们能状况良好地运到你处。

3. 磋商转运或分批

（1）There is no direct sailing between us and transshipment is necessary.

我们之间没有直航,转运是必然的。

（2）The shipping space for the line next month has been booked up. Can we make transshipment via Hong Kong?

下个月这条航线的舱位已经订满了。我们能通过香港转船吗?

（3）We demand partial shipment as you desire earlier delivery.

由于你方想要(我们)提前交货,我们要求分批装运。

（4）What we can do now is to ship the first lot of 20 M/Ts at the beginning of May.

目前我们能做的是在5月初装运第一批20吨的货物。

（5）Due to the fire accident in the warehouse, we cannot deliver the goods in one lot. We wish to make partial shipment.

由于仓库发生火灾,我们不能一次性交货。我们希望分批装运。

七、支 付

1. 请求优惠的支付方式

（1）Since the amount is only 5,000 Euros, can we make payment by T/T?

由于交易金额只有5000欧元,我们可以电汇付款吗?

（2）In view of our long-term cooperation, we propose that payment be made by D/P at sight.

鉴于我们长期合作,我们建议通过即期付款交单付款。

（3）We have been trade partners for years and you assume no risk in accepting our payment terms.

我们多年来一直是贸易伙伴。接受我们的付款条件不会让你们承担任何风险。

（4）We shall appreciate it if you kindly allow us more favorable payment terms.

若能给我们更优惠的付款条件,则不胜感激。

（5）The establishment of L/C means tie-up of funds. Can you accept D/P this time？

开立信用证意味着资金的占压。这次你方能否接受付款交单?

2. 同意对方的支付请求

（1）In view of our past cooperation，we decide to accept your proposal for payment by D/P.

鉴于我们过去的合作，我们决定接受你们付款交单的建议。

（2）Considering the small amount in this transaction，we agree to T/T.

考虑到本次交易金额较小，我们同意电汇付款。

（3）After a careful consideration，we decide to accommodate you with D/P.

经过仔细思考，我们决定予以通融，接受付款交单。

（4）To promote sales in your area，we are willing to accept D/A at 30 days.

为了促进贵地销售，我们愿意接受30天期承兑交单。

（5）We will make an exception this time in view of our past cooperation.

鉴于我们过去的合作，我们这次会破例。

3. 拒绝对方的支付请求

（1）It's our usual practice to make payment by L/C for fresh customers.

对于新客户，信用证付款是惯例。

（2）We are not in a position to accept the proposed terms of payment.

我们不能接受你方提出的支付方式。

（3）Considering the current international situation，it's impossible to accept D/P at this stage.

考虑到当前的国际形势，我们觉得在这个阶段不能接受付款交单。

（4）We will reconsider your requirement for more favorable payment terms after several smooth transactions.

在几次顺利的交易后，我们将重新考虑你方要求，给予更优惠的付款条件。

（5）Your payment conditions are not acceptable. We insist on payment by sight L/C.

你方付款条件不可接受。我们坚持用即期信用证付款。

八、索赔与理赔

1. 索赔

（1）There is a short weight of 20 sets. Could you send them promptly?

（贵司）短交20套，能否尽早发货？

（2）We find the quality of the received goods doesn't match that of the sample.

我们发现收到的货物的品质与样品不匹配。

（3）The goods reached in poor condition and you are held responsible for it.

货物到达时状况不佳，你们应对此负责。

（4）The products are so damaged that they are not marketable.

货物受损严重，没有销路。

（5）We're sorry that you should be responsible for our loss.

很抱歉，你方应对我们的损失负责。

2. 调查

（1）We had a careful check immediately after receiving your letter.

收到贵司来信后，我们立刻进行了仔细检查。

（2）We have conducted a thorough investigation on your complaint.

针对你方的投诉,我们进行了一次彻底调查。

（3）Having investigated the matter carefully, we found it was indeed our fault.

经仔细调查,我们发现错误的确在于我们。

（4）After a careful examination, we found the problem is due to our carelessness.

经过仔细调查,我们发现问题源于我们的粗心大意。

（5）We looked into the matter and apologized sincerely to you for our slip .

我们进行了调查,并为我们的过失向你方真诚地道歉。

3. 理赔或拒赔

（1）We're sorry for the loss incurred and will compensate for your loss accordingly.

我们对所造成的损失深表歉意,并将对你方损失进行相应的赔偿。

（2）We are in receipt of your complaint and will make an early settlement.

我们已经收到贵司投诉,会尽快解决。

（3）The clean L/C shows goods were in good order when they left. Thus, we cannot entertain your claim.

清洁提单表明货物离开时状况良好。因此,我们不能接受你方索赔。

（4）We are sorry to reject your claim as clean B/L has been issued.

由于签发的是清洁提单,所以很抱歉,我们拒绝你方索赔。

（5）The shipping company is responsible for your loss. Therefore, you should contact them to get the problem solved.

船运公司对你们的损失负责。因此,你方应当联系他们解决此事。

📖 学习点拨

外贸业务的实现需要商函作为沟通,有些商函具有**法律效力**(如报价、订购等),所以措辞务必要准确。对于出现的问题,应当本着尊重和理解的态度协商解决,以免影响双方以后的合作。

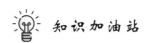 知识加油站

英文猜词法

◎ *利用词缀*。

详见词缀部分知识。

◎ *利用关联词*。

and(并列关系); moreover, besides in addition(递进关系); but, however(转折关系); so, as a result, therefore(因果关系)。

◎ *利用上下文语境*。

例:It's our fault for the loss. We will <u>entertain</u> your claim.

（结合our fault,可以推测出画线单词的意思。）

◎利用生活经验和常识。

例:The selling season is coming. The price is likely to advance.

（根据生活常识,在销售旺季,产品的价格有可能上涨。）

巩固与提升

[真题在线]

句子翻译

1. We regret that _____
（你方价格太高而不能接受). (2012年第89题)

2. We understand your difficult situation, but we regret _____
_____（我方无法考虑你方关于用承兑交单支付的要求). (2013年第88题)

3. We apologize again for this mistake, which must have caused you much inconvenience. (2014年第91题)

4. On the recommendation of Mr. Mark in your area, we are given to understand that you are one of the leading importers of electric goods and wish to establish business relations with us.（2017年第51题）

5. In view of your good reputation, we will make an exception for you and accept payment by Cash against Documents.（2019年第52题）

[强化练习]

句子翻译

1. 我们借此机会与贵司建立业务关系。

2. 原材料价格近期一直在上涨。在此情况下,我们不得不调整我方的报价。

3. AC05型号产品目前断货。我方推荐AC04型号作为替代品。

4. 你方要求提前发货的来信已收悉。目前,我们只能交货50吨。

5. While appreciating your quality, we regret your offer is out of line with the prevailing price.

6. Accepting your present offer means no profit at all. Would you consider a price reduction to some extent?

7. The goods have been ready for shipment. Would you please expedite the establishment of L/C?

8. We apologize to you for the damage to the goods and assure you that your claim will be treated with promptness.

 语法篇

一、形容词和形容词的比较等级

➤ **能力要求**

掌握形容词的基本用法。

掌握形容词比较等级的用法。

➤ **知识储备**

(一)形容词

形容词是用来描写或修饰名词或代词,是用来表示人或事物的性质、特征、状态或属性的词。在句中可以作定语、表语或宾语补足语。

1. 形容词作定语

(1)定语前置　　　　The *growing* demand results in rise in price.

(2)定语后置　　　　The goods *damaged* are useless.

2. 形容词作表语

Their offer remains *competitive*.

3. 形容词作宾语补足语

Our client feels your price *unacceptable*.

(二)形容词的级

形容词有三级变化,即原级、比较级和最高级,表示形容词说明的性质在程度上的不同。

形容词的原级

1. 形容词的原级表示双方在程度上"相等"或"一致",其常用句式如下:

(1)肯定句:A be as +形容词+ as B

(2)否定句:A be not as/so +形容词+ as B

The received products are as good as the sample. 收到的货物与样品一样好。

The old machine is not so efficient as the new one. 旧机器和新机器效率不一样。

2. 形容词原级还可以被程度状语修饰,构成"程度状语+ as + 形容词+ as"句型。

They can supply nearly as much as you. 他们的供应量同你们几乎一样。

3.同级比较时,对象必须要一致。

*Our price is as competitive as **our competitor's**.*

形容词的比较级和最高级

1. 形容词比较级和最高级的构成

（1）规则变化

构成方法	原　级	比较级	最高级
一般单音节词和少数双音节词尾加-er和-est。	low	lower	lowest
以-e结尾的单音节和少数双音节词后加-r和-st。	late	later	latest
重读闭音节末尾只有一个辅音字母时,先双写该辅音字母,再加-er和-est。	thin	thinner	thinnest
以"辅音字母+y"结尾的词,变y为i,再加-er和-est。	busy	busier	busiest
一些双音节词和多音节词在前面加more和most。	fashionable	more fashionable	most fashionable

备注：

A. 双音节形容词比较级和最高级的构成：

① 重音在第一音节的双音节形容词前面加more和most。

famous—more famous—most famous　　　careful—more careful—most careful

② 重音在第二音节的双音节形容词前面加-er和-est。

polite—politer—politest　　　slow-slower—slowest

③ 以-er, -ow, -le, -y结尾的双音节形容词,即使重音在第一个音节,其变化时仍然是在词尾加-er和-est。

simple—simpler—simplest　　　early—earlier—earliest

B. 极少数例外的单音节或双音节词,前面需要加more和most。

real—more real—most real　　　glad—more glad—most glad

C. 由现在分词和过去分词转化而来的形容词的比较等级前面加more和most。

boring—more boring—most boring　　　satisfied—more satisfied—most satisfied

（2）不规则变化

原　级	比较级	最高级
good	better	best
bad	worse	worst
many, much	more	most
far	farther(距离较远的) further(程度较深的)	farthest(距离最远的) furthest(程度最深的)
old	older(年龄较大的,物体较旧的) elder(辈分较大的,资历较深的)	oldest(年龄最大的,物体最旧的) eldest(辈分最大的,资历最深的)
little	less	least

2. 形容词比较等级的用法

（1）形容词比较级用于两者之间在程度、大小、长短、高低及好坏等方面的比较。其常用结构为"A + 形容词比较级 + than + B"。

Our products are more durable than those from neighboring countries.

我们的产品比邻国的产品更耐用。

在比较时，后者经常使用以代词代替与前面相同的成分，请看下面两个句子：

The quality of the received goods doesn't match *that* of the sample.（that代替quality）

The products of your competitor are much better than *those* of yours.（those代替goods）

※归纳：指代单数用that，指代复数用those。

（2）形容词比较级可以被程度状语修饰，构成"程度状语+比较级+ than"结构。程度大的可以用far、much、even、greatly、a lot、a great deal等，程度小的可以使用a bit、a little、a little bit、slightly等。

The arrival date of goods is *far* later than we expected. 货物到达日期远超我们预期。

Our price is *slightly* higher than theirs. 我们的价格只比他们的高一点点。

（3）使用"-er and -er"或"more and more + 形容词原级"表示"越来越……"。

The computer is becoming lighter and lighter. 电脑变得越来越轻了。

Our latest patterns are more and more popular in European Union countries.

我们的最新式样在欧盟国家越来越受欢迎。

（4）"the + 比较级，the + 比较级"表示"越是……就越……"。

The larger the order is, the lower the price will be. 订单越大，价格越低。

（5）比较级也可以用来表示最高级。

We have never seen a better one. 我们没有见到比这个更好的了。

3. 形容词最高级的用法

（1）形容词最高级用于三者或三者以上的比较，表示"最……"，前面一般带有定冠词the，有时候也可以用形容词物主代词代替the。

Our most favorable offer is stated below. 我方最优惠报价如下。

（2）the + 形容词最高级 + 名词 + 定语从句。

The best tea that we purchased is from East China. 我们买过的最好的茶来自华东地区。

（3）one of the + 形容词最高级 + 复数名词 + 范围。

Europe is one of the most important markets in the world. 欧洲市场是世界上最重要的市场之一。

（4）the + 序数词 + 形容词最高级 + 名词。

This is the second most popular type this year. 这是今年第二受欢迎的型号。

形容词的比较级和最高级使用中的特殊情况

1. 形容词比较等级的用法

（1）"the + 比较级"表示两者中"更……的那个"。

Of the two products, we like the bigger one. 这两件产品中，我们喜欢大一点的那件。

（2）除了用than连接比较对象外，一些特殊情况可以用to来连接。

A. "be superior/inferior/senior/junior to"表示"优于、劣于、（资历、年龄、职务等）老于或高于（资历、年龄、职务等）小于或低于。

The received ones are inferior to samples. 收到的产品比样品差。

B. "compare to"用于两者比较。

Compared to other offers, yours is not competitive enough.

同其他报价相比,你方的价格没有足够的竞争力。

2. 形容词最高级的用法

(1)表示事物性质的形容词,没有最高级,如 dead、right、wrong、true、impossible 等。

(2)most 除了用来表示最高级以外,还可以表示"及其,很",相当于"very",用来修饰形容词。

Could you introduce to us a most reliable exporter?

能够向我们介绍一位很可靠的出口商吗?

 学习点拨

形容词的比较等级中,要注意把握好以下三点:一、比较对象的一致性(尤其是代词的使用);二、各种比较等级的结构;三、使用中的几种特殊情况。

一些形容词比较级也可以作动词,如 lower(降低)、further(深化、促进)、better(改善、改良)等,在函电中使用较多。

 知识加油站

本身就是最高级的形容词

complete(完整的)、favorite(最喜欢的)、ideal(理想的)、maximum(最大的)、minimum(最小的)、perfect(完美的)本身就是最高级,不需要再使用 most 或加-est 表示最高级。举例如下:

◎ Goods arrived in perfect condition.

货物到达时状况极佳。

◎ The is the favorite pattern of this year.

这是今年最受欢迎的花式。

◎ This is the maximum concession that we can make.

这是我们能做出的最大让步。

巩固与提升

[真题在线]

一、单项选择题

The quality of our goods is superior _____ those of Indian. (2013年第85题)

A. than   B. with   C. to   D. for

二、句子翻译

1. Transshipment at Hong Kong will enable the goods to reach you earlier as there are more frequent sailings for USA from Hong Kong.（2015年第54题）

2. We have received your products we ordered，but regret to say that they are very much inferior in quality to your samples. Therefore，we ask you to reduce the price by 30%.（2018年第53题）

3. As shipment date stipulated in the L/C is April 30 and cannot be further extended，the goods must be shipped not later than the above date.（2018年第54题）

[强化练习] ···

一、用所给词的正确形式填空

1. This is our _____ catalogue.（late）

2. Could you give us _____ information on product Type A？（much）

3. You price is not competitive enough. We demand a _____ price.（competitive）

4. Of all the products, product A is _____.（popular）

5. FPA is too narrow for goods of this nature. We require a _____ coverage.（broad）

6. The goods received this time can't match _____ of last order.（that）

7. The first business is quite satisfactory to us and _____ orders will follow soon.（far）

8. The raw material is running out. What's _____, the market is declining.（bad）

二、短语翻译

1. at your earliest convenience

2. minimum order

3. outer packing

4. rock-bottom price

5. 内包装

6. 溢短装条款

7. 最大让步

8. 最惠国待遇

三、句子翻译

1. You can contact us for more details on our goods.

2. We will send you a sample for further consideration.

3. Owing to keen competition in the market，the profit is becoming thinner and thinner.

4. Please effect shipment with the least possible delay.

5. 若能优先考虑我们的请求，则不胜感激。

6. 你们竞争对手的报价比你方低5%。

7. 早日开信用证会确保早日发货。

8. 对出口商而言,客户预付货款是最理想的。

二、介 词

➤ **能力要求**

掌握常见介词的具体用法。

掌握介词使用的特殊情形。

➤ **知识储备**

(一)常见介词用法归纳

1. above

(1)表示"位置(在……上面)"

above the bridge

(2)表示"超过(数量,标准,程度)"

above the invoice value

(3)固定搭配

above all

2. after

(1)表示"时间(在……之后)"

after receipt of sth./after sight

(2)表示"持续、反复(一个接一个)"

one after another/day after day

3. against

(1)表示"相反(与……相反;对……不利)"

against the contract

(2)表示"依靠,凭借"

documents against payment/cash against delivery

(3)表示"目的(防备,防止……)"

prepare against the bad weather

(4)表示"位置(在……)"

goods against order No.12

(5)表示"而不是"

We received 35 cases against 40 cases.

4. as

(1)表示"身份(作为……)"

introduce ourselves as... /as an excellent substitute

(2)固定搭配

as usual/as per/as well as

5. at

(1)表示"具体场所,后接小地方"

at the trade fair/at one's end/arrive at Hong Kong

(2)表示"比率、程度(以……速度、价格等)"

at a rate of 5%/at a low price/at your earliest convenience

(3)表示"时间(在……)"

at present/at an early date/at 30 days after sight

(4)固定搭配

at home and abroad/at one's option

6. below

表示"低于(数量、标准、程度)"

below the market level/below the standard

7. between

(1)表示"时间(在……之间)"

shipment between Aug. and Sept.

(2)表示"位置(在……之间)"

between Shanghai and New York

8. by

(1)表示"方式、工具"

by arbitration/by a direct steamer

(2)表示"(时间)不迟于……;在……之前"

by now/by the end of last month

(3)表示"增加或减少的幅度"

raise the price by 3%/reduce the commission by 4%

(4)固定搭配

abide by

9. ex

(1)表示"位置(从……出)"

goods ex M/V "Red Star"

(2)表示"在……交货"

ex works

10. from

表示"位置(来自,源于)"

learn...from.../result from/be available from stock

11. for

(1)表示"时间的持续"

for quite a few years/keep valid for 10 days

(2)表示"目的"

for free distribution/contact us for offers/apply for sth./for one's interest/for one's perusal

(3)表示"原因"

thanks for sth./be obliged for sth.

(4)表示"对象(对于,就……)"

enquire for sth./a big demand for sth./make an offer for sth./place an order for sth./a ready market for sth./good value for money /be ready for shipment

(5)固定短语

for the time being /for one's account/be responsible for

12. in

(1)表示"具体场所"(后接大地方)

in your area/in Asian market

(2)表示"范围(在……内)"

be experienced in/in...line/involve sb. in sth./in...field

(3)表示"方法、手段(用,使用)"

in cash/in dollar

(4)表示"排列、数量(以……形式)"

in good order/in sound condition

(5)表示"时间范围(在……内;在……后)"

in June/in 2021/in coming weeks

(6)固定搭配

in advance/in duplicate/in line with/in large quantities/result in/in one's favor/take pleasure in/ in need of/in possession of/in three equal lots/in transit/result in/in the meantime/in addition to/in reply to

13. into

(1)表示"状态(处于……之中)"

enter into business relations/take sth into. consideration

(2)表示"把……分割为……"

divide sth. into...

(3)固定搭配

look into the matter

14. of

(1)表示"归属"

opening date of the trade fair/name of commodity

(2)表示"事物属性(……的)"

goods of high quality/be of...

（3）固定搭配

free of charge/take advantage of/make use of/consist of/think highly of/be aware of

15. on

（1）表示"基准（在……上）"

be based on/on the basis of/on a reasonable level

（2）表示"一……就"

on receipt of sth. /on arrival of sth. at （...）

（3）表示"对象（关于）"

details on color and size/different opinions on price

（4）固定搭配

on condition that/draw on sb. （a draft）/on our own account/on behalf of sb.

16. out

（1）表示"尽、完"

run out/（be）sold out

（2）表示"状态失常"

out of order

17. out of

（1）表示"范围（在……之外）"

out of line with the market/out of time

（2）表示"缺乏、没有"

out of stock

（3）固定搭配

out of question/out of date

18. over

（1）表示"基准（超过）"

over 500 pieces

（2）固定搭配

all over the world

19. per

（1）表示"每,每一"

8 dollars per set

（2）表示"位置（装在……）"

goods per s/s "Red Star"

（3）表示"按照"

per S/C = as per S/C

20. plus

表示"加上,附加"

invoice value plus 10%

21. than

表示"比较(用于比较级)"

more than 3000 pieces/lower than others

22. through

(1)表示"凭借,经由(媒介、方法)"

through the courtesy of sb./through fax

(2)表示"经历,历经"

through 50 years' experience/go through difficulties

(3)表示"时间(在整个期间)"

through the year

23. till

表示"直到……为止"

work till late/till now

24. to

(1)表示"位置(向……,朝……)"

direct inquiries to/look forward to/draw one's attention to/owe...to...

(2)表示"动作的对象(对于……)"

be of interest to sb./be acceptable to sb.

(3)表示"动作的对象(场所,程度)"

advance...to.../extend...to...

(4)表示"时间、数目(到,到……为止)"

from March to July/cut the price to 10 *yuan*/yard

(5)独立用法(充当副词)

to one's regret/satisfaction/surprise

(6)固定搭配

subject to/due to/owing to/to some extent/appeal to/come to terms/give priority to

25. under

(1)表示"隶属关系(在……之下)"

under the circumstance/come under our scope/goods under order No.123

(2)表示"位置(在……之下)"

under separate cover

(3)表示"基准(低于、少于)"

orders under 1000 yards

(4)表示"状态(在……中)"

under discussion

26. up

(1)表示"朝……上方"

go up

（2）固定搭配

build up business relations/tie up funds/check up/book up

27. via

（1）表示"位置（经由，通过）"

transshipment via Hong Kong

（2）表示"方式（凭借，通过）"

contact sb. via e-mail

28. with

（1）表示"伴随（与……一起）"

establish business relations with sb./do business with sb./open an account with sb./place an order with sb./cooperate with sb./compare with sth.

（2）表示"方式（以……，用……）"

leave us with small profit/accommodate sb with sth.

（3）固定短语

be satisfied with/with keen interest/with reference to

29. within

表示"时间、位置（在……内部）"

within the stipulated time/within the area

30. without

表示"没有"

without delay/without hesitation/without engagement

（二）介词使用特殊情况

介词组合

1. Looking forward *to* hearing *from* you soon *with* keen interest.

2. look *for* a supplier *as* trade partner *at* your end

3. They wish to enter *into* business relations *with* us *in* the line *of* shoes.

4. Thanks *for* your interest *in* purchasing 3,000 sets *of* Color TVs.

5. Please quote us *for* 1,000 sets *of* air conditioners *on* FOB Ningbo basis *with* shipment *in* April.

6. *At* your request, we are making you an offer *for* goods Item No.05 as follows, subject *to* your reply reaching us *in* ten days.

7. We will allow you a discount *of* 5% *on* orders *for* 5,000 pieces or above.

8. Please cut the price *by* 10% *per* piece *in* view *of* our relations.

9. place an order *for* cloth *with* us *at* 10 dollars/piece

10. cover the goods *for* 110% *of* invoice value *against* All Risks

11. effect insurance *on* 2,000 cases *of* goods *for* our account

12. effect insurance *on* the goods *for* 10% *above* the invoice amount *with* PICC

13. send you *by* return mail the pamphlet *regarding* the scope *of* cover handled *by* PICC

14. apply *for* survey *to* the survey agent *without* delay

15. book shipping space *for* your order *for* 30 cases *of* shoes *per* s/s victory

16. to be effected *within* 30 days *after* receipt *of* L/C.

17. The shipping space *for* the line has been booked *up till* November.

18. ship the goods *as* a trial *to* us *by* D/P *at* sight

19. open an L/C *at* 30 days *through* a bank acceptable *to* us

20. L/C is to reach us *by* the end *of* this month valid *for* negotiation *in* china until the 15th day *after* date of shipment.

21. lodge a claim *against* sb. *on* sth. *for* money

22. make an apology *to* you *for* the inconvenience caused *by* us

介词误用

1. 收到某人某日的来信

receive a letter on + 日期(×)

receive a letter of + 日期(√)

2. 通过某人的推荐

through the recommendation of sb. (×)

on the the recommendation of sb. (√)

3. 在某人的帮助下

under the help of sb. (×)

with the help of sb. (√)

4. 比……优/劣

be superior/inferior than...(×)

be superior/inferior to...(√)

5. 为货物投保

cover insurance for the goods（×）

cover insurance on the goods（√）

6. 在香港转运

transshipment in Hong Kong（×）

transshipment at Hong Kong（√）

7. 信用证的修改

amendment of L/C（×）

amendment to L/C（√）

8. 向某人索赔

lodge a claim to sb.（×）

lodge a claim against sb.（√）

9. 尽早，尽快

on an early date（×）

at an early date（√）

介词通用

1. 在……时间内

in ten days = within ten days

2. 一收到……

on receipt of = upon receipt of

3. 订单上的货物

goods under Order No. 01 = goods against Order No.01= goods in Order No. 01

4. (船只)开往某地

sail for... = sail to...

5. 在某处转运

transshipment at Hong Kong = transshipment via Hong Kong

6. 通过第三方

open an L/C with a bank = open an L/C through a bank

7. (……上的)条款

stipulations in... = stipulations of...

8. 投诉(某物)

complain about sth. = complain of sth.

9. (数量)达到……

Amount is to $ 5,000. = Amount is up to $ 5,000.

10. 通过邮件

contact us through email = contact us by email

11. 至于,关于

as for sth. = as to sth.

12. 历经,持续

through the year = throughout the year

13. 在三者或三者以上

among the goods = amongst the goods

14. 几分之几

two in three = two out of three

 学习点拨

介词是前置词,表示名词、代词等与句中其他词的关系,在句中**不能单独作句子成分**。

介词后面一般有名词、代词或相当于名词的其他词类、短语或从句作它的宾语,表示与其他成分的关系。**如果后面跟动词短语的话,要把动词处理成其动名词形式。**

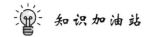 知识加油站

介词与其他词类搭配

类　型		举　例
动词与介词	动词+介词	agree with, conform to
	动词+名词+介词	take advantage of, draw attention to
	动词+副词+介词	look forward to, add up to
形容词与介词	be +形容词+介词	be pleased with, be consistent with
名词与介词	名词+介词	in stock, by collection
	名词+介词+名词	day after day, step by step
	介词+名词+介词	by means of, with regard to

巩固与提升

[真题在线]

单项选择题

1. We cannot supply the order because it is _____ stock. （2011年第66题）

　　A. from　　　　　　B. out　　　　　　C. out of　　　　　　D. in

2. We'd like to apologize _____ our customers _____ the poor quality of machine tools. （2012年第69题）

　　A.to, of　　　　　　B. for, in　　　　　　C. to, for　　　　　　D. with, of

3. Please inform us _____ your terms of payment. （2013年第60题）

　　A. of　　　　　　B. on　　　　　　C.to　　　　　　D. in

4. We are sending you _____ separate cover our latest price list. （2014年第60题）

　　A. in　　　　　　B.by　　　　　　C. under　　　　　　D. to

5. We complained _____ the seller _____ the short weight. （2014年第69题）

　　A. of, to　　　　　　B. about, for　　　　　　C. of, about　　　　　　D. to, of

6. We owe your name and address _____ the Commercial Counselor's Office of the Australia Embassy in Beijing. （2015年第29题）

　　A.at　　　　　　B. to　　　　　　C. from　　　　　　D.in

7. We can't dispatch the goods this month because the shipping space for the line has been fully _____ until the end of March. （2016年第37题）

　　A. booked off　　　　　　B. booked in　　　　　　C. booked up　　　　　　D. booked with

8. Since we have only 7 metric tons of green tea _____ stock, we can only make you this offer subject _____ prior sale. (2017年第32题)

　　A.in, on　　　　　　　B. on, in　　　　　　　C. in, to　　　　　　　D. on, to

9. Your Panda Brand TV Sets appeal to us. Please quote your best prices _____ various specifications on CIF Singapore basis. (2018年第29题)

　　A. in　　　　　　　　B. of　　　　　　　　C. for　　　　　　　　D.to

10. We should be obliged if you could furnish us _____ a complete report _____ the credit standing of the mentioned company. (2019年第31题)

　　A. on, for　　　　　　B. for, on　　　　　　C.with, on　　　　　　D.with, for

［强化练习］

一、单项选择题

1. The L/C No. BD24 is _____ favor of JBL Company.

　　A. with　　　　　　　B. of　　　　　　　　C. in　　　　　　　　D. on

2. We look forward _____ your information_____ this respect.

　　A. to, at　　　　　　　B. for, in　　　　　　　C. to, in　　　　　　　D. for, at

3. Your letter _____ May 6th was received, _____ which we note you desire to trade with us.

　　A. on, with　　　　　　B. of, at　　　　　　　C. on, of　　　　　　　D. of, through

4. There is steady demand here _____ cotton piece goods _____ high quality.

　　A. in, of　　　　　　　B. for, of　　　　　　　C. for, for　　　　　　　D. of, of

5. Our end-users complain _____ the inferior quality _____ us.

　　A. about, to　　　　　B. about, against　　　C. against, with　　　D. against, about

6. As instructed, we will draw _____ you a sight draft for collection through the Bank of China.

　　A. for　　　　　　　　B. against　　　　　　　C. on　　　　　　　　D. from

7. _____ the 200 TVs under Contract No. 456 we shall cover insurance ourselves.

　　A. On　　　　　　　　B. In　　　　　　　　C. By　　　　　　　　D. For

8. We place this order_____the understanding that the discount is 5%.

　　A. with　　　　　　　B. at　　　　　　　　C. through　　　　　　　D. on

9. We suggest that your order_____ a minimum order quantity of 8,000 pieces.

　　A. call on　　　　　　B. call in　　　　　　　C. call for　　　　　　　D. call up

10. The cost has been _____ the rise, so we are forced to raise the price _____ 3%.

　　A. in; by　　　　　　　B. on; by　　　　　　　C. in; to　　　　　　　D. on; to

二、介词填空

1. We contacted the shipping company _____ receiving your letter.

2. Unless you reduce your price _____ $2.5 per yard, we see no possibility of business.

3. The goods are _____ sale and soon they will be sold _____ .

4. The goods can be covered _____ a rate of 0.8%.

5. _____ S/C No. BD26, goods will be shipped _____ three equal lots.

6. We await _____ keen interest your reply.

7. The shipping company is responsible _____ the loss and you should lodge a claim _____ them.

8. We looked _____ the matter and found the mistake is due _____ our carelessness.

9. Our clients are in urgent need _____ the products and appreciate your delivery _____ delay.

10. The goods enquired _____ are out of stock and we recommend AC05 _____ an excellent substitute.

三、非谓语动词

➤ 能力要求

了解非谓语动词的种类及其在句子中的位置。

掌握非谓语动词在句子中的用途。

➤ 知识储备

非谓语动词是指句子中除了谓语动词以外的动词形式。非谓语动词分三类:动词不定式、动名词和分词(现在分词和过去分词)。

(一)动词不定式

动词不定式的结构为 to do 或 to be,它有时态和语态的变化,具体见下表(以动词 do 为例)。不定式的否定结构为 not + to do/be。

时态语态	主 动	被 动
一般时	to do	to be done
进行时	to be doing	—
完成时	to have done	to have been done

不定式在句子中除了不能充当谓语外,可以担当其他成分。

1. 不定式作主语

当不定式或不定式短语充当句子主语时,指代一件事,谓语动词要用**单数**。

To develop a new market is rather difficult. 开拓一个新市场相当困难。

To finish unloading the goods in one day seems unlikely. 一天内卸完货看上去不太可能。

不定式作主语时常常用形式主语 it 代替,上述两句可以调整如下:

It is rather difficult to develop a new market.

It seems unlikely to finish unloading the goods in one day.

这种结构可以归纳为一个句型:It is + adj. + (for sb) to do sth.

It is necessary for seller to investigate the credit of buyer before doing business.

在做生意前,卖家调查买家的资信很有必要。

在这个句型中,形容词用来表示事物的特征或特点,是一种客观事实,常用形容词有 difficult、

important、impossible、necessary、urgent等。如果形容词用来表示人物的性格特点、品格等,是一种主观情感或态度,则使用It is + adj. + of sb. to do sth.句型。

It's considerate of the seller to use the water-proof material to pack the goods.

使用防水材料包装产品,卖方真是考虑周到。

2. 不定式作宾语

They failed to meet our order. 他们不能满足我方订单。

We decide not to initiate the business with them. 我们决定不同他们开启交易。

搭配不定式的常见动词有 advise、agree、attempt、afford、arrange、begin、decide、desire、demand、expect、fail、hesitate、hope、intend、manage、mean(打算)、promise、propose、refuse、start、wish等。

如果不定式短语较长,在句子中可以用it作形式宾语来代替不定式。

We find it impossible to allow you a discount in this case.

我们觉得在这种情况下不能给予折扣。

3. 不定式作宾语补足语

They advise us to accept T/T. 他们建议我方接受电汇。

使用"动词+ sb. to do sth."结构的动词还有 ask、encourage、expect、force、get、wish等。

4. 不定式作表语

The best way now is to apologize. 目前最好的办法是道歉。

5. 不定式作定语

The attempt to make direct contact failed. 建立直接联系的尝试失败了。

不定式作定语通常位于所修饰的名词后。

6. 不定式作状语

To simplify procedure, we hope to make payment by T/T this time. (目的状语)

为了简化手续,我们希望这次通过电汇付款。

We are pleased to meet you at the fair. (原因状语)

很高兴在展会上遇到您。

We received the products this morning, only to find they are not for us. (结果状语)

我们今早收到了货物,发现货物不是我们(订购)的。

7. 使用不定式的一些固定结构或句型

(1)too...to... 太……以至于……

Your price is too high to be acceptable. 贵司价格太高,我们无法接受。

(2)have no choice but to do sth. 别无他法只得做某事

The seller had no choice but to raise the price. 卖家别无他法,只得提价。

8. to有两种用法,一种是本章节提到的to do,还有一种是to为介词,后面接名词或动名词,如be/get used to sth/doing sth.(习惯于做某事)、with a view to doing sth. (为了做某事)、attach sth. to sth. (把……附着于……)等。

(二)动名词

动名词兼有动词和名词特征的非限定动词。它具备名词的特征,可以在句中作主语、宾语、表语及定语。

它有时态和语态的变化,具体见下表(以动词 do 为例)。它的否定结构为 not + doing/being。

时态语态	主　动	被　动
一般时	doing	being done
完成时	having done	having been done

1. 动名词作主语

Doing international business requires language ability and trade skills.

从事国际贸易需要语言能力和贸易知识。

不定式和动名词都可以作主语,前者一般表示具体的、一次性的动作,而后者一般表示抽象的、经常或习惯性的动作。

To collect information on AB Company's credit is not easy. 收集 AB 公司资信信息不容易。

Collecting market information is of great importance. 收集市场信息极其重要。

动名词作主语时,有时可以使用 it 作形式主语,将动名词置于句末。

It is no good/use doing sth. 做某事无济于事/没有作用。

2. 动名词作宾语

(1)跟在及物动词后作宾语

这些及物动词有 admit、allow、appreciate、avoid、consider、delay、deny、dislike、enjoy、finish、forbid、mean(意味着)、keep、permit、risk、suggest 等。

We won't delay shipping the products you need. 我们不会耽误发送你们需要的货物。

We don't want to risk buying them at present. 我们目前不想冒险采购它们。

(2)跟在介词后作宾语

They are desirous of importing our goods. 他们渴望进口我们的产品。

He came to visit our factory without informing us. 他没有通知就来我们工厂参观。

(3)跟在一些动词词组后面作宾语

can't help doing sth. 情不自禁做某事

give up doing sth. 放弃做某事

insist on doing sth. 坚持做某事

put off doing sth. 推迟做某事

3. 动名词作表语

动名词作表语时常表示无生命的事物。主语和后面的表语通常是对等的关系,可以相互交换位置。

Your task is packing the goods. = Packing the goods is your task. 你的任务是包装货物。

4. 动名词作定语

packing material = material which is used for packing 包装材料

动名词作定语一般用于表示修饰物的用途和性能。

5. 动名词的逻辑主语

动名词的逻辑主语(动作的发出者)一般由名词的所有格(sb's)或物主代词(my、your、his、her、their、our)充当。它和后面的名词构成一个复合结构。

We anticipate your sending us a sample. 期待贵司给我们寄送样品。

（三）分词

分词分为现在分词（doing）和过去分词（done）。

现在分词有时态和语态的变化变化，具体请见下表，但过去分词没有这些变化。它的否定结构只需要在分词前加 not 即可。

时态语态	主 动	被 动
一般时	doing	being done
完成时	having done	having been done

分词在句中一般作定语、表语、补语和状语。

1. 分词作定语

a confirming bank 保兑行   a confirmed L/C 保兑的信用证

a developing country 发展中国家   a developed country 发达国家

现在分词表示一个主动的、正在进行的动作或行为，表示事物的性质和特征；过去分词表示一个被动的、已经完成的动作或行为。

2. 分词作表语

Your products are interesting, so our clients are very interested.

你们的产品有吸引力，我们的客人很有兴趣。

现在分词作表语，主语一般为事物；过去分词作表语，主语一般为人。

3. 分词作补语

We found two cartons missing. 我们发现少了两箱。

We hope to have the goods repacked. 我们希望将货物重新包装。

4. 分词作状语

（1）现在分词作状语

Considering the quality, you will feel our offer realistic.（条件状语）

如果考虑品质的话，你会觉得我方报价符合实际。

Not knowing your specific requirement, we cannot make a firm offer.（原因状语）

由于我方不知道贵司的具体要求，我们不能报实盘。

Not having received any reply to our email, we decided to send another one.（原因状语）

由于我们没有收到对我方邮件的任何回复，我们决定再发一封邮件。

Having been checked for three times, the sample was sent this morning.

被检查了三次以后，样品今早发出。

（2）过去分词作状语

Given more discount, we will consider a trial order.（条件状语）

如果你们给我们更多折扣，我们会考虑下一个试订单。

📖 学习点拨

非谓语动词在句子中可以充当多种成分,它有时态和语态的变化(过去分词 done 除外)。它们搭配的动词也比较固定,如搭配不定式的动词可以整成顺口溜:三个希望(hope,wish,expect)两答应(promise,agree),两个要求(require,request)莫拒绝(refuse)。设法(manage)学会(learn)做决定(decide),不要假装(pretend)在选择(choose)。

非谓语的否定形式为“not + 非谓语”,但是要注意,现在分词的完成否定结构为“not having done”,不是“having not done”。

 知识加油站

有些动词既可以搭配不定式,也可以搭配动名词。搭配以后,意思有些没有变化,如 like 和 start;有些则变化明显,如 mean 等。下面将搭配后意思发生变化的情况做一个归纳:

verb + to do sth.	verb + doing sth.
1. forget to do sth. 忘记去做某事(未做)	1. forget doing sth. 忘记做过某事(已做)
2. go on to do sth. 做了一件事后,接着做另一件事	2. go on doing sth. 停顿以后,继续做原来做的事
3. regret to do sth. 对要做的事表示遗憾	3. regret doing sth. 对做过的事表示遗憾
4. remember to do sth. 记得要去做某事	4. remember doing sth. 记得做过某事
5. stop to do sth. 中断某事去做另一件事	5. stop doing sth. 停止做某事
6. try to do sth. 企图做某事	6. try doing sth. 试着做某事

巩固与提升

[真题在线]

一、单项选择题

1. With a view _____ the market in your city, we have offered you our bottom price.(2011 年第 69 题)

    A. to promote   B. to promoting   C. of promote   D. into promote

2. We are making you this offer, subject to your reply _____ here on or before May 16.(2012 年第 63 题)

    A. reach   B. reaching   C. reaches   D. reached

3. If any article interests you, please don't hesitate _____ us.(2015 年第 30 题)

    A. contacting   B. having contacted   C. to contact   D. to have contacted

4. Chinese costumes for ladies are increasingly popular in Malaysia for the time being, so we are considering _____ some of them.（2015年第31题）

    A. import   B. to import   C. importing   D. being imported

5. _____ to my manager about your proposal, we agree to accept payment by T/T.（2016年第38题）

    A. Talked   B. Talking   C. Having talked   D. Being talked

6. We have pleasure in enclosing a _____ pricelist for the goods you _____ in your letter. （2019年第29题）

    A. detail, informed   B. detailed, said   C. detail, told   D. detailed, required

二、翻译下列句子或短语

1. 催促某人做某事（2014年第75题）

2. _____（为了避免日后修改），please make sure the stipulations of L/C are in accordance with terms and conditions of the contract.（2014年第88题）

3. 为了鼓励我们之间的生意,我方愿意提供给贵方一个总金额5%的特别折扣。（2019年第56题写作）

4. 很高兴收到你方10月6日的邮件（2020年第56题写作）

［强化练习］

一、用所给词的正确形式填空

1. We are interested _____ some of your products.（import）

2. Accepting your current prices _____ losing money.（mean）

3. Our trade partner advises us _____ early decision as market is advancing.（make）

4. They have no choice but _____ us for the loss incurred.（compensate）

5. We are sorry for _____ the goods in a wrong way.（pack）

6. They desire to have the price _____.（adjust）

7. She was _____ with our products and services.（satisfy）

8. _____ to expand the business in East Europe, we decided to set up a branch there.（aim）

二、单项选择题

1. They won't risk _____ your goods at so high a price.

    A. purchase   B. to purchase   C. purchasing   D. purchased

2. We try to persuade them_____ our proposal, but they insist on _____ to theirs.

    A. to accept, adhere   B. to accept, adhering

    C. accepting, adhering   D. accepting, to adhere

3. The result remains _____ and we would rather _____ for another two days.

    A. unknown, wait   B. unknown, to wait

    C. not knowing, wait   D. not knowing, to wait

4. _____ in 1990, they enjoy a good fame worldwide.

    A. Being established   B. Establishing   C. Established   D. Having established

5. _____ more trade practices and you will find it easier to do international trade.

    A. To know   B. Knowing   C. Know   D. Known

6. _____ our goods with other brands, you will find they are good value for money.

    A. To compare   B. Comparing   C. Compared   D. Being compared

7. He is a nice sales assistant and always does what he can _____ others

    A. help   B. helping   C. to help   D. helps

8. We wish, for both interests, them _____ the price to some extent.

    A. reduce   B. reducing   C. reduced   D. to reduce

三、句子翻译

1. 开立信用证会占压我方很多资金。

2. 请尽力在规定时间内将货物发出。

3. 请避免犯同样的错误。

4. 我们别无他法只好将受损的货物退回。

5. 为了将贵司的损失最小化，我们会尽快把问题解决。

6. 不断上涨的价格迫使我们相应涨价，期待能得到您的理解。

7. 不想被市场淘汰，他们打算在6月推出新产品。

8. 同供货商协商了好几次，我们终于拿到了期待已久的价格。

四、句子成分和简单句的五种句型

➤ 能力要求

了解句子的八种成分：主语、谓语、表语、宾语、宾语补足语、定语、状语和同位语。
掌握五种常见简单句基本句型。

➤ 知识储备

(一)句子成分

1. 主语

主语是句子叙述的主体，一般位于句首，但在 there be 句型、疑问句(主语不是疑问代词)和倒装句中，主语位于谓语、助动词或情态动词后面。主语可由名词、代词、数词、不定式、动名词短语和主语从句等来充当。

Mobile phones sell well here.（名词）

He is our regular customer.（代词）

One third of the received goods were greatly damaged.（数词）

To accept your offer means loss.（不定式）

It is impossible to lower the price.（it作形式主语,真正的主语为不定式）

Expanding business in a new market is not easy.（动名词短语）

What we need is sample.（主语从句）

2. 谓语

谓语用于说明主语所做的动作或具有的特征和状态,位于主语之后,一般由动词充当。

We handle leather shoes.（及物动词）

The selling price increases.（不及物动词）

They are interested in our scarf.（动词短语）

We will consider your proposal.（情态动词加动词）

E&M Co. has received a few inquiries lately.（助动词加动词）

3. 表语

表语用于说明主语的性质、特征和状态,一般位于be动词(am、is、are)、感官动词(look、sound、smell、feel、taste)、特殊系动词(seem、appear、prove、grow、remain、get、become、turn out)之后。通常由名词、代词、形容词、分词、数词、不定式、动名词、介词短语、副词和表语从句充当。

This is our latest design.（名词）

Our offer remains valid in ten days.（形容词）

One carton was damaged.（分词）

The biggest problem is to book shipping space.（不定式）

The goods are in good order.（介词短语）

More business is ahead.（副词）

The problem is where to find a new supplier.（表语从句）

※ prove/turn out/appear/seem后面除了跟形容词,也可接不定式,尤其是to be短语作表语。

The business proves to be profitable.

The goods turn out to be satisfactory.

4. 宾语

宾语表示动作的对象和承受者,一般位于及物动词和介词后面。通常由名词、代词、数词、不定式、动名词短语和宾语从句充当。

We export textiles.（名词）

They will send us free sample.（代词）

The importer decides to trade with us.（不定式）

We are considering purchasing 20 M/Ts .（动名词短语）

We look forward to what we need.（宾语从句）

5. 宾语补足语

英语中,一些及物动词除了有一个宾语外,还需要一个宾语补足语,才能使句子的意义完整。宾语补足语可以由名词、形容词、副词、不定式、分词、介词短语来充当。

We name our brand victory.（名词）

Our clients think the offer unworkable.（形容词）

It is air-tight. Don't let the air in.（副词）

The rising costs force us to adjust the price.（不定式）

He saw them discussing the shipping schedule.（现在分词）

We noticed the received goods in poor condition.（介词短语）

※ have作动词，表示"让某人/某物……"时，其宾语补足语有三种动词形式，使用时需要仔细分析：

have the workers（to）pack the goods（to do中的to一般省略）

have the machine working all night（doing）

have the goods loaded on board（done）

6. 定语

修饰名词、代词的词、短语或从句称之为定语。可以由名词、形容词、数量词、代词、不定式、分词、动名词、介词短语和从句来充当。

The table cloth sells well.（名词）

We require a realistic price.（形容词）

Three suppliers are in the room.（数量词，冠词）

We have a problem to deal with.（不定式）

The rising cost makes them unhappy.（现在分词）

We won't accept damaged goods.（过去分词）

They need washing machines of high quality.（动名词，介词短语）

We are searching a company exporting shoes.（动名词短语）

Would you give some information on their credit?（介词短语）

The goods which are ready for shipment were ruined.（定语从句）

7. 状语

修饰动词、形容词、副词或整个句子，用于说明动作或状态特征的句子成分称之为状语。它可以位于句首，也可以位于句中和句尾。可由以下形式表示：

We will do it accordingly.（副词）

The latest style is widely accepted in the US market.（副词、介词短语）

To conclude our first business, we will reduce the price.（不定式）

Not having received a reply, we decided to write again.（分词短语）

They won't place an order unless there is a 5% discount.（状语从句）

※ 状语可以分为以下几类：

Last year, our sales volume totaled 80,000 euros.（时间状语）

H&K is our agent in Europe.（地点状语）

Due to the rising costs, we have to adjust the selling price.（原因状语）

He insists on making payment by documents against payment.（方式状语）

We will allow you a special discount to initiate our first business.（目的状语）

Our products are superior to those from other sources.（比较状语）

The goods are so damaged <u>that they are useless</u> .（结果状语）

<u>Negotiating with his counterpart</u>，he wrote something important down.（伴随状语）

8. 同位语

一个名词(或其他形式)对另一个名词或代词进行解释或补充说明,这个名词(或其他形式)就是同位语。同位语与被它限定的词的格式要一致,并常常紧挨在一起。

ABC Corporation，<u>our long-term partner</u>，will attend the fair.（主语的同位语）

They will introduce Mr. Wang，<u>a leading buyer</u>，to us.（宾语的同位语）

The fact <u>that you have not effected shipment</u> troubled us.（同位语从句）

※ 引导同位语从句的一般是抽象意义的词，如 news、fact、information、idea、message、proposal、suggestion等。

(二)五种句型

1. 主语 + 谓语(S+V)

句型特点:谓语动词为不及物动词,本身能表达完整的意思,后面不需要跟宾语,但有时候可以跟副词和介词短语作状语。

The market declined.

The selling price rises by 5%.

2. 主语+ 系动词+ 表语(S+V+P)

句型特点:谓语动词为系动词,不能表达完整的意思,后面需要跟上一个表明主语特征、身份、状态的表语。

The price remains unchanged.

The business is profitable.

3. 主语 + 谓语 + 宾语(S+V+O)

句型特点:谓语动词为及物动词,不能单独完整表达意思,须跟一个宾语。

They are signing a contract.

The manufacturer raises the wholesale price.

4. 主语 + 谓语 + 宾语 + 宾语(S+V+O+O)

句型特点:谓语动词为及物动词,后面跟两个宾语,它们都是动作的对象或承受者。前一个为间接宾语,后一个为直接宾语(真正意义上的宾语)。

Kindly airmail <u>us</u>(间接宾语)<u>your lowest price</u>(直接宾语).

We will allow <u>them</u>(间接宾语)<u>a 5% discount</u>(直接宾语).

※ 也可以把直接宾语提前到间接宾语之间,通常需要加介词for或to。

They passed an specific enquiry to us yesterday.

5. 主语 + 谓语 + 宾语 + 补语(S+V+O+C)

句型特点:谓语动词为及物动词,后面跟了一个宾语,但意思不够完整,必须再加上一个补语,对宾语进行补充说明。

We find your price <u>acceptable</u>.

We heard them <u>discussing the shipping schedule</u>.

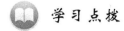 **学习点拨**

　　句子翻译时,首先找出句子的**主干部分**(主语和谓语)和次要部分(宾语、定语及状语等)。其次,把握好**时态**和**语态**。最后,注意**拼写**、**句子结构**及**标点符号**等细节。

　　句子翻译是否贴切、合理,需要注意语境,更要注意措辞的**准确性**和商函的**专业性**,并把握好商务基本礼仪规则。

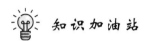 **知识加油站**

介词短语作状语时在句子中的位置

一般位于句首和句尾:

<u>At present</u>, there is a strong demand in EU market.

Shipment was delayed <u>as a result of the bad weather on sea</u>.

有时也会移动到句中,这时句子的理解难度有所增加:

Thank you **in advance** for your cooperation.

We await **with keen interest** your reply.

Kindly open **with a bank** a confirmed irrevocable L/C.

Would you be kind enough to obtain **for us** the information?

巩固与提升

[真题在线]

一、单项选择题

1. The L/C stipulation should be in _____ accordance with the terms _____ the Contact. (2011年第68题)

　　A. exact, for　　　　　B. the same, on　　　　C. exactly, of　　　　D. exact, of

2. Our customers are _____ with your goods. (2012年第61题)

　　A. satisfactory　　　　B. satisfy　　　　　　C. satisfied　　　　　D. satisfaction

3. Complying _____ the request in your E-mail dated May 17, we are sending you our _____. (2014年第64题)

　　A. to, quote　　　　　B. with, quote　　　　C. to, quotations　　　D. with, quotations

4. If you should _____ able to reduce your price _____ 5%, we could probably come into business. (2017年第30题)

　　A. been, by　　　　　B. be, by　　　　　　C. been, off　　　　　D. be, off

二、句子翻译

1. 我们同意接受你方的全部索赔要求。(2013年第89题)

2. 我们不可能再降价了。(2014年第89题)

3. 关于我方的财务状况和可靠性,请向中国银行杭州分行查询。(2016年第49题)

4. 买方凭检验证明书向卖方提出索赔。(2017年第50题)

[强化练习]

一、单项选择题

1. Would you please _____ us favorable terms of payment in this deal?

    A. extend   B. expand   C. intend   D. pretend

2. We feel your offer _____ as the market is declining.

    A. acceptance   B. unaccepted   C. unacceptably   D. unacceptable

3. _____ troubles us most is the shortage of raw material.

    A. It   B. That   C. What   D. This

4. They promise to avoid _____ such similar mistake in the future.

    A. to make   B. making   C. make   D. made

5. We would like to know whether our price is _____ to you.

    A. agreement   B. agreed   C. agreeable   D. agreeably

6. As the market is advancing, we are forced to raise the price _____.

    A. urgently   B. seriously   C. accordingly   D. frequently

二、用横线画出句子中的相应成分

1. We will remit you the full value by T/T. (直接宾语)

2. The risk can be covered at a rate of 0.5%. (谓语)

3. Where to find a reliable supplier remains a problem. (主语)

4. Our first cooperation proves profitable. (表语)

5. Please have the L/C established in the prescribed time. (宾语补足语)

6. The goods dispatched is for our long-term partner, S&H Brothers. (同位语)

三、用所给词的正确形式填空

1. Please keep us _____ of what's going on at your end. (inform)

2. We appreciate _____ sending us an early reply. (you)

3. _____ an L/C will tie up our funds for a long time. (open)

4. The goods of this pattern _____ well. (sell)

5. PICC enjoys a high reputation in _____ claims equitably and promptly. (settle)

6. It is of mutual benefit for both parties _____ a contract. (sign)

7. We are _____ of importing some sports shoes. (desire)

8. Please note the _____ date of L/C is approaching. (expire)

五、时 态

► **能力要求**

掌握常见的四大时态(过去时、现在时、将来时、完成时)。

掌握表示将来时的特殊情况。

了解将来完成时的用法。

► **知识储备**

(一)一般现在时

一般现在时主要强调一种事实,经常发生的动作或状态。句子中经常出现表示频率的副词,如 usually、always、occasionally。在使用的过程中,当主语是第三人称单数时,注意要做到主谓一致。

They sell stainless kitchenware. 他们销售不锈钢餐具。

ABC Co. is our exclusive agent in North America. ABC公司是我们在北美的独家代理。

动词第三人称单数变化规则:

◇ 一般情况下,动词后面直接加"s",例:claim→claims, enter→enters。

◇ 以 ch-、sh-、s、x、o 结尾的动词,在后面加"es",例:match→matches, finish→finishes, dismiss→dismisses, fax→faxes, do→does。

◇ 以辅音字母加y结尾的动词,把y变为i,加"es",例:comply→complies, supply→supplies。

◇ 以元音字母加y结尾的动词后面直接加"s",例:delay→delays, survey→surveys。

在由 when, after, before, till, as soon as, the minute/moment 等引导的时间状语中 if, as long as, provided(that), on condition that, once, even if, in case 等引导的条件状语中,主句用一般将来时,从句常用一般现在时代替一般将来时,也就是我们经常所说的"主将从现"。

We will grant you a 3% discount if your order <u>exceeds</u> 800 cartons.

如果你们订单超过800箱,我们将给予3%的折扣。

Once fresh goods <u>come in</u>, we will contact you immediately.

一旦到货,我们会立刻联系你们。

转移性动词,如 come, go, arrive, leave, start, begin 等的一般现在时可以用来表示将来,主要用来表示时间已经确定好或安排好的事情。

The vessel leaves this Sunday. 这艘船周日离开。

The trade fair starts next Monday. 交易会下周一开始。

(二)一般过去时

一般过去时表示过去的动作和状态,也可以表示过去某一段时间内经常或反复出现的动作。句子中会出现 last month/year、then、two years ago 及 in the past 等表示过去的时间状语。一般过去时往往通过动词的过去时来体现。动词的变化分为两类:一类为规则动词,变化规则如下;另一类为不规则动词,需要强化记忆。

规则动词过去时变化规则:

◇ 一般情况直接加"ed",例:load→loaded, obtain→obtained。

◇ 以不发音的字母 e 结尾的动词,在其后直接加"d",例:enable→enabled, insure→insured。

◇ 以辅音字母加 y 结尾的动词,把 y 变为 i,加"ed",例:carry→carried, notify→notified。

◇ 以元音字母加 y 结尾的动词,在其后直接加"ed",例:delay→delayed, survey→surveyed。

◇ 以重读闭音节结尾的动词,双写最后的辅音字母加"ed",例:commit→committed, refer→referred。

We obtained your name from the last trade fair. 我们从上次的交易会上获取你方名号。

They signed a contract last week. 他们上周签了合同。

表示在过去一段时间内,经常性或习惯性的动作。

When I was responsible for export, I usually went to the customs.

在一些固定句型中,我们也通常会使用过去时。

◇ It's(high)time that sb. did sth..表示"到了某人做某事的时间了"。

It's high time that we discussed terms of payment. 我们该谈谈支付方式了。

◇ It's/has been...since...表示"自从……以来,已有多少时间了"。since 前一般用一般现在时或现在完成时,since 后一般用过去时。

It is/has been three days since we made the complaint. 我们投诉已经过了三天了。

◇ ...was/were doing sth when...did sth...表示"正在做某事,这时突然……"。

We were packing the goods when she stepped in.
我们在包装货物的时候,她走了进来。

(三)一般将来时

一般将来时表示将要发生的动作或存在的状态,常与表示将来的时间状语连用,如 tomorrow、next Monday/week/month、in(the)future、in two weeks 等。它的结构如下:

结　构	运　用
will + do/be	一般都用这个结构;可以用于表示客观事实的新闻报道。
be going to + do/be	表示事先商定、安排或打算要去做的事情。
be + to do	按照要求、规定必须或应该要去做的事,在法律条文、商务信函中使用较多。
be about to do	表示即将要发生的事情,一个动作即将发生的时候另一件事发生了。

The trade fair will take place next month. 交易会下个月举行。

We are going to dispatch the goods this Friday. 我们打算本周五发货。

Insurance is to be covered by seller since the trade is concluded on CIF basis.

由于交易以CIF术语达成,保险应当由卖家办理。

The ship is about to leave when a storm hits. 船即将开出之际,一场暴风雨来临。

"shall+ 动词原形"也可以表示将来。shall前的主语一般为第一人称I和we,表示承诺、征求意见、委婉等,但有时也可以是第三人称,表示说话者的意图、告诫、威胁、命令、决心等,在正式的文件、文章中表示义务或规定。

The goods shall be sent within the stipulated time. 货物应当在规定的时间内发送。

(四)现在进行时

现在进行时一般用于表示现在正在进行的动作或状态,常与表示现在的时间状语连用,如at present、now、at the moment、right now、currently等。它的结构为"be + 现在分词",be同主语保持一致。

现在分词的变化规则:

◇ 一般动词后面直接加"-ing",例:request→requesting, sell→selling。

◇ 以不发音的e结尾的单词,去掉不发音的e加"-ing",例:issue→issuing, urge→urging。

◇ 以y结尾的动词后面直接加"ing",例: apply→applying, survey→surveying。

◇ 以重读闭音节结尾的动词,双写最后的辅音字母加"-ing",例:cut→cutting, plan→planning。

◇ 特殊变化:

die→dying   lie→lying   tie→tying   be→being

They are negotiating the payment terms at present. 他们目前正在协商支付方式。

The policy is being prepared. 保单在准备之中。

现在进行时使用时的几种特殊情况:

◇ 有些动词不能用在进行时中,主要分为以下五类:五个拥有或从属(have、possess、own、consist、belong)、四个感官动词(feel、look、seem、sound)、四种情感(like、love、hate、want)、四个思维(think、believe、understand、know)和三个存在(exist、remain、stay)

◇ 当句子涉及明确的计划、安排或意图时,可以使用现在进行时表示一般将来时。

They are flying to Hamburg to attend a trade fair next Monday.

他们下周一飞往汉堡参加一场交易会。

◇ 现在进行时有时可以用来表示满意、称赞、惊讶、厌恶等感情色彩,句子中通常与always、forever、continually、constantly等副词连用。

She is constantly making mistakes. 她总是犯错误。(表示厌恶)

(五)现在完成时

现在完成时表示过去发生或已经完成的动作对现在造成的影响或结果,或从过去已经开始,持续到现在的动作或状态。它的结构为"have/has + 过去分词"。常用的时间状语有already、ever、never、yet、just、so far、recently、up to now、lately、for + 一段时间、since + 过去的时间点、in the past weeks/months/years等。

We have been in the line for 20 years. 我们从事该行有20年了。

Up to now, we still have not received his response. 到目前为止,我们尚未收到他的回应。

在一些固定句型中,我们也通常会使用现在完成时。

◇ It is the first/second time that...结构,从句部分需要使用完成时。

It is the first time that both parties have agreed on payment.

这是双方第一次就支付达成一致。

◇ This is the +形容词最高级+ that...结构,从句部分需要使用完成时。

This is the highest offer that we have received. 这是(目前为止)我们收到的最高报价。

◇ must + have done结构,表示对发生在过去事实的肯定推测。

The goods left here in quite good condition. The damage must have taken place in transit.

货物离开时状况非常良好。损坏一定是发生在运输途中。

(六)过去完成时

过去完成时是表示在过去某一时间或某一动作之前已经发生或完成的动作或事情。它表示的是发生在"过去的过去"的动作,句子中一般有很明显的参照动作或时间状语,其结构是"had +过去分词"。过去完成时句中常见的时间状语有before、by the end of +过去时间点。

We had packed the goods before they called. 在他们打电话之前,我们已经完成包装了。

By the end of last week,we had sold 2,000 copies. 截止到上周末,我们已售出 2000 份。

过去完成时经常使用在以下两种情况中:

◇ 在 told、said、knew、heard、thought 等动词后的宾语从句。

She informed us that she had received the sample. 她通知我们说她已经收到样品了。

◇ 在时间状语从句中,对于不同的时间发生的两个动作,发生在前的动作,用过去完成时;发生在后的动作,用一般过去时。

When the goods arrived,the deadline had exceeded. 货物到达时,已经过截止日期了。

在特定句型中,我们也通常会使用过去时。

◇ No sooner...than.../Hardly...when... 表示"一(刚)……就……"。这是个部分倒装结构,than/when 的前面用过去完成时,后面用一般过去时。

No sooner <u>had</u> the vessel <u>left</u> than the storm came. 船刚离开暴风雨就来临了。

Hardly <u>had</u> they <u>finished</u> loading when a fire accident happened. 他们刚装完货火灾就发生了。

(七)过去将来时

过去将来时表示从过去某个时间来看将要发生的动作或存在的状态,常用于宾语从句或间接引语中,其常用"would + 动词原形"或"was/were going to + 动词原形"来表示。

We did not know whether we would attend the next trade fair. 我们不知道是否会参加下一届交易会。

She said that she was going to fly to New York. 她说她要飞往纽约。

它也可以在虚拟语气中使用:

◇ If引导的虚拟语气,同现在的情况相反,主句使用过去将来时。

If I were you, I <u>would accept</u> the price. 如果我是你,我就会接受这个价格。

◇ wish引导的虚拟语气,表示将来不太会实现的事情。

We wish you <u>would lower</u> the price. 要是你们能降价就好了。

(八)现在完成进行时

现在完成进行时表示动作从过去某一时间开始,一直延续到现在,可能还要继续下去。其结构为 "have/has been + 动词的现在分词",强调动作的延续性。

They have been working for 3 hours, but they still haven't finished it.

他们已经持续工作3个小时了,但仍未完成。

它还可以运用在以下两种情况:

◇ 强调动作延续时间的长久或带感情色彩。

As a salesperson, she has been working hard to develop new markets.

作为一名销售,她一直努力开拓新市场。

◇ 表示以前这段时间反复发生的事情。

They have been sending mails to each other recently. 他们最近一直有信件来往。

 学习点拨

时态的选用需要综合多种因素:一、句子中的时间状语或时间状语从句;二、句子的语境;三、表达习惯或固定用法。如将来时有多种形式,但当在商函中要表示"按照要求、规定必须或应该要去做的事"时,一般使用"be + to do"结构。

时态的变化主要体现在动词的变化上,一些特殊变化需要特别留意,如重读闭音节结尾的双写、以"y"结尾的动词等。

 知识加油站

函电中"已经"的几种不同时态

◎ 表示目前的状态时,可以用一般现在时。

例:我们已经收到贵司的传真。

We **are** in receipt/possession of your fax.

◎ 表示事情或动作已经结束,可以用一般过去时。(注意时间状语)

例:他们昨天已经发货了。

They **dispatched** the goods <u>yesterday</u>.

◎ 表示动作已经结束,使用现在完成时。(强调结果或当前的状态)

例:货物已平安到达我处。

The goods **have reached** us safely.

◎ 表示事情在过去某一时间节点已经结束,需要使用过去完成时。(注意时间状语)

例:截止到上周五,我们已经收到20个订单。

We **had received** 20 orders <u>by the end of last Friday</u>.

巩固与提升

句子翻译

1. We hope you will establish the relevant L/C before the end of this month. （2012年第91题）

2. 信用证一个星期左右可以到达你方。（2015年第56题写作）

3. 若你方订货不迟于本月底，我们保证即期装运。（2016年第56题写作）

4. 考虑到及时交货，我们不得不通知贵方第238号订单货物已经备妥待运，但是至今我们还未收到相关信用证。（2019年第50题）

[强化练习]

一、单项选择题

1. We shall advise you by cable as soon as the goods _____.
   A. will ship   B. were shipped   C. will be shipped   D. are shipped

2. We are sorry for the short weight by 5 tons. This _____ you some trouble in meeting the demand of your clients.
   A. must have caused   B. will cause
   C. has been caused   D. can be caused

3. Once the supplies _____, we will contact you immediately.
   A. will come in   B. come in   C. came in   D. have come in

4. They didn't ship the goods per s/s "Swan", because they _____ to book the shipping space.
   A. fail   B. failed   C. had failed   D. have failed

5. We _____ the insurance policy and it will be sent in a week.
   A. prepare   B. are preparing   C. have prepared   D. prepared

6. They _____ the examination of all goods by the end of this month.
   A. finish   B. will finish   C. had finished   D. will have finished

7. We learned from your fax today that our laptops haven't reached you. They _____ on May 10th and should have reached you.
   A. dispatched   B. have dispatched   C. will dispatch   D. were dispatched

8. We are not in a position to accept your counter-offer as market _____.
   A. advances   B. is advancing   C. advanced   D. have advanced

9. I'm writing to inform you that the goods against your Order No. 7556 _____ ready for shipment, but we _____ your relevant L/C. （2017年37题）

A. were; did not receive   B. were; have not yet received

C. have been; did not receive   D. have been; have not yet received

二、句子翻译

1. 你们的全力配合会让我们不胜感激。

2. 收到你们的投诉信后,我们就联系了船公司。

3. 直到现在,我们还是没收到你们对于延误的解释。

4. 相信你们会对我们的产品和服务满意。

5. 他们正在会议室协商支付方式。

6. 在双方多次讨论以后,卖方最终决定在价格上做出让步。

7. 我们一直以来向你们提供质高价优的产品。

8. 货物三周前离开这里,现在肯定到达目的港了。

六、被动语态

➤ 能力要求

掌握常见时态的被动语态。

掌握使役动词、宾语补足语、双宾语、动词短语等情况下的被动语态。

掌握主动表被动的几种情况。

➤ 知识储备

被动语态是动词的一种特殊方式,表示句中的主语是动作的承受者,因此谓语动词必须是及物动词。其结构为"be + 过去分词",其中be有时态、人称和数的变化。

(一)被动语态的用法

◇ 当我们不知道谁是动作的执行者,或没有必要指出是谁。

All the products are made in our factory.

◇ 强调动作的承受者。

Trade fair was held last year.

（二）主动语态转化为被动语态步骤

◇ 把主动语态句中的主语变为被动语态句中的"by + 物/人的宾格"。

◇ 把主动语态句中的宾语变为被动语态句中的主语。

◇ 把主动语态句中的谓语的核心动词变为"be +过去分词"。

◇ 检查被动语态句子的时态、主谓、标点符号等是否同主动语态句子一致。

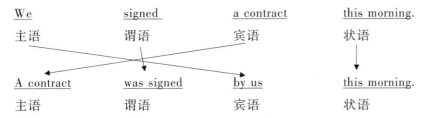

（三）常见时态主动语态与被动语态的对比

下面以动词 send 为例，在基本时态中体现：

时　态	主动语态	被动语态
一般现在时	We send the goods.	The goods are sent by us.
一般过去时	We sent the goods.	The goods were sent by us.
现在进行时	We are sending the goods.	The goods are being sent by us.
一般将来时	We will send the goods. We are to send the goods.	The goods will be sent by us. The goods are to be sent by us.
现在完成时	We have sent the goods.	The goods have been sent by us.
过去完成时	We had sent the goods.	The goods had been sent by us.
将来完成时	We will have sent the goods.	The goods will have been sent by us.

（四）几种特殊情况的被动语态

◇ 谓语动词为使役动词(let、make、have)时，主动变为被动时，在第二个动词前加上"to"。

Our boss makes us work 10 hours a day.（主动）

We are made **to** work 10 hours a day by our boss.（被动）

◇ 谓语动词中含有情态动词的，把谓语动词变为"情态动词 + be done"。

You should open the L/C at once.（主动）

The L/C should be opened at once（by you）.（被动）

◇ 句子中含有宾语补足语时，只需要按照原来的变化规则，宾语补足语跟在"be + done"后。

We urged them to make punctual shipment.（主动）

They were urged to make punctual shipment by us.（被动）

They think our offer unreasonable.（主动）

Our offer is thought unreasonable by them.（被动）

◇ 句子中含有双宾语变为被动时，有两种办法，其中直接宾语作主语时，间接宾语前通常加介词"to"。

They faxed us a confirmation yesterday. （主动）

We were faxed a confirmation by them yesterday. （被动,间接宾语作主语）

A confirmation was faxed **to** us by them yesterday. （被动,直接宾语作主语）

◇ 及物动词构成的动词短语,如"动词 + 介词""动词 + 副词"等,在变被动结构时,要把它们看成一个整体,不能分开。

They take advantage of this opportunity. （主动）

This opportunity is taken advantage of by them. （被动）

（五）没有被动语态的情况

◇ 不及物动词和不及物动词词组不能用于被动语态,如 occur、take place、exist、arrive、reach、appear、come true、break out、sail for 等。

◇ 表示属于的动词,如 have、own、belong to 等。

◇ 表示希望、意图的动词,如 wish、hope、want 等。

◇ 宾语是反身代词或互相代词时,一般不能用被动语态。

（六）主动语态表示被动语态的几种情况

◇ 表示事物本身的属性的动词。

The goods sell well. 货物畅销。

The cloth lasts long. 这布经久耐用。

◇ 谓语动词为感官动词时,一般用主动表示被动。

It feels soft. 它摸起来很软。

The cake tastes good. 蛋糕尝起来很不错。

◇ 谓语动词为 need 或 require 表示"需求、需要"时,后面跟 doing,可以用来表示被动。

The commodity needs/requires checking. 商品需要检验。

◇ 用"be worth doing"表示"做某事时值得的"。

The product is worth buying. 货物值得购买。

◇ 用"under + 名词"表示"事物正处在……状态之中"。

The warehouse is under construction. 仓库正在建设中。

The payment terms are under discussion. 支付方式正在讨论之中。

（七）一些常用被动的结构和句型

◇ "as + 被动"表示"按照……,如……那样"。

as requested/stated/stipulated/contracted

◇ 主语从句"It's + 过去分词+ that…"。

It's expected that... （预计……）

It's estimated that... （据估计……）

学习点拨

　　被动语态相对于主动语态存在,在实际中运用广泛。在使用时,动作的发出者经常省略,谓语动词必须为及物动词或及物动词构成的短语。在使用时,注意把握好主谓一致原则。

　　个别动词在使用时可能出现两种情况,如:sell well(畅销)没有被动语态,但是(be) sold out(售罄)则要使用被动语态。一些动词的被动语态也会出现两种情形,如:上文提到的 need、require、want 表示"需要"时,既可以用"need/require/want + doing",也可以使用"need/require/want + to be done"结构表示被动。对于这些特殊情况,我们要特别关注。

知识加油站

一般疑问句如何变为被动

◎ 首先把一般疑问句变为陈述句。(调整为陈述句语序:主语 + 谓语 + 宾语 + 其他)

◎ 再把上述陈述句变为被动语态。(变化规则:参看本章相关内容)

◎ 最后把变为被动句的陈述句变为一般疑问句。(be 动词、助动词或情态动词提到句首)

例 1: Can they provide silk goods?(一般疑问句)

They can provide silk goods.(陈述句)

Silk goods can be provided by them.(陈述句改为被动语态)

Can silk goods be provided by them?(将上一步骤的句子改为一般疑问句,与原句呼应)

例 2: Did he sign the contract yesterday?

He signed the contract yesterday.(注意要把 do、does 和 did 同动词融合,变成一个词)

The contract was signed by him yesterday.

Was the contract signed by him yesterday?

例 3: Have they checked the goods?

They have checked the goods.

The goods have been checked by them?

Have the goods been checked by them?

巩固与提升

[真题在线]

一、单项选择题

1. Your name and address _____ to us by your Chamber of Commerce.(2011年第62题)

　　A. have been given　　　　B. give　　　　C. have given　　　　D. be given

2. According to the contract, insurance should be _____ by the buyer.（2012年第68题）

    A. cover   B. covering   C. coverage   D. covered

3. Many of the bags _____, and we reserve the right to claim damages.（2013年第68题）

    A. were damaging   B. were damaged   C. was damaging   D. was damaged

4. It is stipulated in the S/C that insurance on goods shall _____ by seller for 110% of the invoice value.（2014年第68题）

    A. covered   B. is covered   C. be covered   D. cover

5. With reference to our S/C No. PTS 12 for 1,000 pieces of Men's shirts, which are _____ from Ningbo to Sydney by S/S China Star tomorrow, we would like you to effect insurance.（2015年第37题）

    A. to ship   B.to be shipping   C. to be shipped   D. to have shipped

二、句子翻译

1. In the event of loss or damage which may result in a claim under this policy, immediate notice must be given to the company or agent as mentioned in the Policy.（2015年第53题）

2. 合同规定以你方为受益人的信用证已经通过中国银行宁波分行开立。（2015年第56题）

3. As the shipment date stipulated in the L/C is April 30 and cannot be further extended, the goods must be shipped not later than the above date.（2018年第54题）

[强化练习] --

一、单项选择题

1. When will the goods _____?

    A. are delivered   B. deliver   C. be delivered   D. delivery

2. As per the Order No.126, the shipment _____ in May.

    A. is made   B. will be make

    C. is to be made   D. has been made

3. We have the goods _____ before _____ them.

    A. checked, sent   B. checking, sending

    C. checked, sending   D. checking, sent

4. All the goods _____, and we will deliver them without delay.

    A. is packed   B. was packed   C. have packed   D. have been packed

5. We are glad to inform you that the first batch of goods _____.

    A. was sold out   B. sold out   C. was sold well   D. were sold out

6. Please note that delivery will be _____ within three months after _____ of your order.

    A. make, receipt   B. made, receiving   C. make, receiving   D. made, receipt

7. Our new designs _____ in EU market.

    A. think highly   B. think highly of

    C. are thought highly   D. are thought highly of

8. It is _____ that extra expense shall be _____ by us.

    A. understanding, borne   B. understood, borne

    C. understanding, bearing   D. understood, bearing

二、将下列句子的主动语态变为被动语态

1. A customs officer is checking the leather bags.

2. We must deliver the goods before the end of this month.

3. They haven't received any reply yet.

4. We will fax you our lowest quotation soon.

5. Our clients found your price unrealistic.

6. Will you insure the goods on our behalf?

三、句子翻译

1. 信用证已由开证行开出。

2. 文件保存在哪里啊?

3. 合同正在准备中。

4. 信件发出之前应该先让总经理签名。

5. 卖方被要求不得晚于10月1日交货。

6. 你们需要的样品将另寄。

7. 货物在运输途中受损严重,不能出售。

8. 我们可以给予你方特殊折扣,条件是订单须在两周内到达我处。

七、定语从句

➤ **能力要求**

了解定语从句的种类。

掌握定语从句中关系代词及关系副词的用法。

➤ **知识储备**

定语从句本质上是定语,用来修饰名词或代词。被修饰的名词或代词称为先行词,定语从句位于先行词之后,由关系代词或关系副词引导。

定语从句分为两类:限制性定语从句和非限制性定语从句。主要区别有两点:形式上,主句和从句之间没有逗号隔开的是限制性定语从句,有逗号隔开的是非限制性定语从句;意思上,限制性定语从句中,从句同先行词关系紧密,非限制性定语从句中,从句同先行词关系不太紧密。

<u>The trade partner</u>（who exports shoes）is from East China.（限制性定语从句）

（先行词）　　　　　　　　（从句）

<u>The vessel</u>,（which sails for Amsterdam tomorrow）,is now at the port.（非限制性定语从句）

（先行词）　　　　　　　　（从句）

（一）定语从句常见句型

1. 限制性定语从句

……先行词(从句)

先行词(从句)……

2. 非限制性定语从句

……先行词,(从句)

先行词,(从句),……

3. 特殊情况(用 which 或 as 指代一个句子)

一个句子,which/as...

As...,一个句子。

（二）关系代词和关系副词

1. 关系代词

关系代词	先行词	在从句中的成分	能否省略
who	人	主语	不能省略
whom	人	宾语	可以省略
		宾语	介词的宾语且前置时,不能省略
whose	人或物	定语	不能省略

关系代词	先行词	在从句中的成分	能否省略
which	物	主语	不能省略
		宾语	可以省略
		宾语	介词的宾语且前置时,不能省略
	整个主句	主语	不能省略
that	人或物	主语	不能省略
	人或物	宾语	可以省略
	人和物	主语	不能省略
as	整个主句	主语	不能省略

who：We need a partner who can supply stationery.

我们需要一位能够供应文具的伙伴。

whom：The agent (whom) we appointed last month sent us an e-mail.

我们上月任命的代理昨天发来了邮件。

They contacted Mr Wang, with whom we have traded for years.

他们联系了王先生,我们同王先生做了很多年的生意。

whose：The importer needs goods whose quality is high.

进口商需要品质高的产品。

We are looking for a salesperson whose English is excellent.

我们正在寻找一位英语极佳的销售人员。

which：The sample, which arrived this morning, is satisfactory to us.

样品今早到达,让我们满意。

They sent us the catalog (which) we requested.

他们给我们邮寄了我们需要的样品。

This is a problem with which we have to cautiously deal.

这是一个需要我们谨慎处理的问题。

The exporter suddenly raised the price, which made us surprised.

出口商突然涨价,这让我们很吃惊。

that：The person that sells goods to a foreign country is called exporter.

将货物出售给国外的人被称为出口商。

The letter that urges us to advance shipment is from our regular customer.

催促我们提早发货的信件来自老顾客。

The person (that) we just met is our exclusive agent.

我们刚刚遇见的那个人是我们的独家代理。

We consider importing the new machine (that) they are now using.

我们考虑进口他们正在使用的新机器。

Trade partners and failures that helped me grow won't be forgotten easily.

帮助我成长的贸易伙伴和种种失利是不会被轻易遗忘的。

as：As you see, the market is advancing. 如你所见, 行情正在看涨。

备注:

◇ 先行词出如果是公司、银行等, 需仔细区分。如果它指代的是这些机构本身, 要用 that 或 which；如果它指代的是这些机构里面的具体的经办人, 要使用 who 或 whom。

The company, <u>which</u> was founded in 1998, is a leading one in the line. (which 指公司)

You can contact Bank of China, from <u>whom</u> you can know our credit. (whom 指银行工作人员)

◇ which 指代整句内容时, 一般位于句中；as 指代整句内容时, 既可以位于句中, 也可以位于句首。

The goods of Chinese origin are very popular, which is known to all.

原产于中国的产品深受欢迎, 这是众所周知的。

As you know, our goods sell well. 如你所知, 我们的产品畅销。

Our goods sell well, as is known to all. 我们的产品畅销, 这是众所周知的。

◇ as 除了指代整个主句以外, 还可以作宾语, 运用在 the same...as、such...as 等固定句型中。

They export the same product as we do. 他们出口和我们一样的产品。

◇ 只能用 that 作关系代词的情况。

当先行词是不定代词时, 如 all、few、little、much、something、anything、everything 等。

Is there anything（that）we can do for you?

当先行词被 the only、the very、the same、little、few、no、any 等修饰时。

This is the only order that exceeds 20 M/Ts.

当先行词被序数词或形容词最高级修饰。

The best price（that）we can quote is as follows.

2. 关系副词

关系副词	先行词	在从句中的成分	副词可以替换为
when	时间	时间状语	介词 + which
where	地点	地点状语	介词 + which
why	the reason	原因状语	for + which

when: Could you let us know the date when/on which the trade fair will start?

能否告知交易会开始的日期?

where: This is the warehouse where/in which they store raw materials.

这是他们储存原材料的仓库。

why: That's the reason why/for which their goods are so salable.

那就是他们的产品如此畅销的原因。

备注:

◇ 时间、地点作先行词时, 要注意区分它们在从句中充当的成分。如果是主语和宾语, 要使用 that 和 which(用法具体参见上面关系代词)；如果作时间状语和地点状语, 要用 when 和 where。

◇ why 作为关系副词, 必须由先行词 the reason 来引导, 它在从句中充当原因状语, 但是当 the reason 在从句中充当主语或宾语时, 就不能用 why 了。

Do you know the reason which he gave? (你知道他给出的理由吗?)

◇ why表示原因也可以用于表语从句,试比较下面一组句子:

That's the reason why their goods are so salable. (定语从句,从句修饰先行词the reason。)

这就是他们的产品如此畅销的原因。

That's why their goods are so salable. (表语从句,why引导的从句作is的表语。)

这就是他们的产品如此畅销的原因。

(三)介词 + which/whom

先行词同从句连接时,有时候需要使用介词。定语从句中介词的选择要注意把握两个原则:

1. 固定搭配原则

This is the reason **for** which shipment was delayed. (why = for which)

This price, **of** which you can make full use, is realistic. (make full use of sth.)

2. 句意通顺原则

Please send us the shipping documents, **without** which it's impossible to take delivery.

请寄送装运单据,没有提单便无法提货。

We believe you will accept our price, **at** which many transactions have been concluded.

我们相信你方会接受我们的价格,很多交易以这个价格达成。

备注:先行词在从句中充当时间状语或地点状语时,需要用when或where来引导,也可以用"介词 + which"来替。我们需要根据先行词和句意,选择合适的介词。

The goods must reach us in March, when/**by** which our stock will run low. (by表示截止到)

The goods reached the port of destination, where/**at** which they were waiting. (at +小地方)

(四)常见错误

1. 主谓不一致

(1)先行词理解有误导致不一致。

This is one of the products which **interests** us. (×)

This is one of the products which **interest** us. (√)

(先行词是products,是复数,谓语动词interests应当改为interest。)

This is the only one of the products which **were** imported. (×)

This is the only one of the products which **was** imported. (√)

(先行词是the only one of the products,是单数,谓语动词were应当改为was。)

(2)先行词在从句中充当主语,但由于主句被从句分割,有时候没有把握主谓一致。

The products (which you're interested in) **is** out of stock. (×)

The products (which you 're interested in) **are** out of stock. (√)

2. 代词与关系代词混淆

(1)it/which

We quoted you an offer, it will remain valid for 10 days. (×)

We quoted you an offer, **which** will remain valid for 10 days. (√)

(2)they/who

You can contact suppliers in China, they will provide silk in large quantities. (×)

You can contact suppliers in China, **who** will provide silk in large quantities. (√)

（3）them/whom

They have two agents, both of them are reliable. (×)

They have two agents, both of **whom** are reliable. (√)

3. 先行词没有找准

当先行词是时间或地点，且前面有介词时，误把先行词看成介词短语，导致关系词使用错误。

They finally arrived at the warehouse, which finished products are stored. (×)

（先行词是 warehouse 不是 at the warehouse，所以用 where。）

📖 学习点拨

在限制性定语从句中，从句位于先行词之后，且不能分割，不可能出现下面这种情况：

The goods sell well (which are made of fine material). (×)

　　先行词　　　　　　　　　从句

应当改为：

The goods (which are made of fine material) sell well. (√)

　　先行词　　　　　　　定语从句

当先行词在从句中充当主语，且后面有 be 动词时，通常可以省略关系代词和 be 动词。

原句：The L/C which is in favor of ABC Company was issued yesterday.

省略后：The L/C in favor of ABC Company was issued yesterday.

 知识加油站

如何选用关系代词或关系副词

◎ 确定先行词属于何种类型，人、物、人和物（that）抑或是整个句子。

◎ 分析从句缺少何种成分，以从**句中的谓语动词**为突破口，利用十字方针——"主谓、动宾、动状、介宾和修饰"，确定先行词在从句中的成分。如：

The goods, _____ arrived yesterday, are satisfactory to us.

（从句只有谓语动词 arrived，缺少主语，先行词作主语。）

We received the sample _____ you sent last week.

（从句的谓语动词 sent 为及物动词，缺少宾语，先行词作宾语。）

They went to the meeting room _____ they would have a business negotiation.

（从句结构和意思完整，考虑增加状语，表示动作的地点，先行词作状语。）

Can you send us a catalog covering the goods _____ we are interested in.

（从句有主语和谓语，谓语动词为含介词的短语，缺少宾语，先行词作宾语。）

The products, _____ quality is high, are selling fast.

（从句结构和意思完整，且先行词不能充当状语，可以考虑先行词是否修饰从句的主语，先行词作定语。）

◎ 根据句意，关系代词前有时候需要加相应的介词，构成介词 + which/whom 结构。

巩固与提升

一、单项选择题

You were recommended to our company by the Bank of China, New York Branch, _____ told us _____ you export Chinese table cloths. (2013年第67题)

    A. that, which   B. which, that   C. what, that   D. that, what

二、句子翻译

1. We apologize again for this mistake, which must have caused you some inconvenience. (2015年第91题)

2. 我们的付款方式通常是以保兑的、不可撤销的、按发票金额见票即付的信用证支付,该信用证应通过我们认可的银行开出。(2016年第50题)

[强化练习]

一、单项选择题

1. We learn your name from DEC, _____ has traded with us for years.

    A. that   B. it   C. what   D. which

2. This is our lowest price, _____ many deals are closed.

    A. that   B. at it   C. which   D. at which

3. We will consider cooperating with suppliers _____ quotations are attractive.

    A. which   B. who   C. whose   D. whom

4. We are indeed sorry _____ the goods _____ are out of stock.

    A. that; which you enquired   B. that; which you enquired for

    C. that; that you enquired   D. which; that you enquired for

5. We are now sending you the contract in duplicate, a copy of _____ please countersign and return to us for record.

    A. which   B. them   C. those   D. these

6. They are now expanding their business in West Africa, _____ people need goods of high quality at competitive prices.

    A. which   B. at which   C. where   D. there

7. Was it in this room _____ two parties signed the contract?

    A. which   B. it which   C. where   D. that

8. The best thing _____ we can do is _____ the goods available to you.

    A. which; dispatching   B. what; dispatching

    C. which; to dispatch   D. /; to dispatch

二、在横线处填上合适的介词

1. The goods under Order No.28CD arrived yesterday, _____ which our clients are satisfied.

2. This is the latest offer, _____ which we believe you will make full use.

3. Bank of China, Ningbo is our banker, _____ which you can refer for our credit.

4. This is the reason _____ which they complain about the goods.

5. The fax, _____ which you can clearly know our position, was sent yesterday.

6. Allen Hardson, _____ whom we have done business for years, visited our company.

7. The B/L is important, _____ which it is impossible to take delivery of goods.

8. We are now talking to a manufacturer, the price _____ whom is quite reasonable.

三、句子翻译

1. We are in receipt of your mail dated June 20, for which we thank you.

2. This is our final decision, which will remain unchanged.

3. The goods reaches us later than the expected time, which has caused us much inconvenience.

4. They recommend us to introduce our products to Southeast Asia, where there is a growing demand due to the development of economy.

5. 请联系货代，他们会派货车去取货。

6. 请尽快开立信用证，一收到该证我们会安排及时发货。

7. 货物到达时状况不佳，你们应该对此负责。

8. 火灾损坏了原材料，这让我们遭受了巨大的损失。

八、状语从句

► 能力要求

了解状语从句的种类。
掌握状语从句中常用的关联词。

► 知识储备

状语从句，顾名思义就是用一个句子来充当状语。它的功能等同于状语，可以分为时间状语从句、地点状语从句、方式状语从句、原因状语从句、结果状语从句、条件状语从句、比较状语从句、目的状语从句和让步状语从句九种。

（一）时间状语从句

时间状语从句通常用来说明主句动作发生的时间。常用的引导词有 when、as、while（当……时）、before（在……之前）、after（在……之后）、since（自从……）、until/till（直到……）、as soon as/the moment/the minute（一……就）。

1. 引导词区分

（1）when、as 和 while 的区别

when 引导的时间状语从句中的动词既可以是短暂性动词也可以是延续性动词，运用较广。as 侧重表示从句和主句的动作同时发生，意为"一边……，一边……"。while 引导的时间状语从句中的动作必须是延续性动词，强调主句和从句的动作同时发生。

When Christmas season comes, the sales will increase.

当圣诞季到来的时候，销路会增长。

As time went by, he found more and more clients.

随着时间的推移，他找到了越来越多的客户。

While they were manufacturing the goods, we were loading the goods.

当他们生产产品时，我们在装货。

（2）until 和 till 的区别

使用 until 引导句子时，主句一般含有否定词 not，构成"not...until..."，而 till 前一般没有否定词，意思上没有明显差别。

They didn't reply until we wrote the second time. 直到我们第二次写信他们才回复。

We kept pressing them till the L/C was opened. 我们一直在催促他们直到信用证开立为止。

2. 句子时态

（1）一般情况下，从句一般使用一般现在时，主句使用一般将来时。

We will send you an offer as soon as we receive your specific enquiry.

一收到你方具体询盘，我们就会向你们报价。

When all the things are ready, they will contact you. 等到一切就绪，他们会联系你。

（2）while 作引导词时，从句部分一般使用进行时态，主句时态则需要根据实际情况确定。若主句和从句的主语一致，从句可以省略主语和 be 动词。

An accident occurred while they were packing. 当他们在包装时，发生了一起事故。

Please give us details on colors while (you are) quoting. 报价时，请告知颜色细节。

（3）since 作引导词表示"自从……"时，句子时态请参考语法章节的时态部分。

3. 特殊情况

while 除了表示"当……时"，还可以用来表示对比，相当于 although，常位于句首。

While we find your quality satisfactory, your price seems unacceptable.

尽管我们觉得你们的质量令人满意，但是你们的价格似乎令人难以接受。

（二）地点状语从句

在句中作地点状语的从句被称为地点状语从句。常用的引导词为 where 和 wherever。

Where there is a will, there is a way. 有志者，事竟成。

He will go wherever business is possible. 他会到任何有生意可做的地方去。

(三)方式状语从句

方式状语从句一般用 as if、as though 引导,意为"似乎,好像",多使用虚拟语气。

He **speaks** as if he *knew* nothing about it.

(四)原因状语从句

原因状语从句通常用来说明主句动作发生的原因。常用的引导词有 because、as、since 和 for。 because 回答 why 提出的问题,表示直接的因果关系,语气强烈;as 引导的从句语气比 because 弱;since 含有"既然"的意思,常放于主句之前,表示已知或明显的原因,翻译时甚至可以省略;for 语气最弱,通常位于主句之后作补充说明,主句和从句间有逗号隔开。

We suffered huge loss because you made a mistake. 由于你犯了错误,我们损失巨大。

As there is no direct vessel, we have to persuade our customer to accept transshipment.
由于没有直达船,我们不得不说服客户接受转船。

Since we are your regular customer, you assume no risk in accepting our proposal.
我们是你们的老客户,接受我们的建议不会让你们承担任何风险。

It's wise to cut the price, for other suppliers have already lowered the price.
其他供货商已经下调价格了,降价是明智之举。

(五)结果状语从句

用于表示结果的状语从句称为结果状语从句,常用的结构为:such/so...that...。

(1)such 的用法

① such + a/an + adj. + 可数名词单数 + that...

He is such a reliable partner that we can trust him.

他是一个可靠的伙伴,我们可以相信他。

② such + adj. + 不可数名词 + that...

Your goods are of such poor quality that we won't accept them.

你们产品的品质如此低劣,我们无法接受。

③ such + adj. + 可数名词复数 + that...

They can provide such various patterns that our customers show great interest.

他们可以提供众多款式,我方客户表现出了很大的兴趣。

(2)so 的用法

① so+ adj. + a/an + 可数名词单数 + that...

The product has so unique a design that they decide to place an order.

产品拥有独特的设计,所以他们决定订购。

② so+ many/few + 可数名词复数 + that...

They received so many orders that they will be busy in the coming weeks.

他们收到了很多的订单,未来几周会很忙。

③ so + much/little + 不可数名词 + that...

The transaction involves so much amount that the seller insists on payment by L/C.

该笔交易牵涉的金额很多,卖方坚持要信用证付款。

※ 当little意为"小"时,要用such.

It is such a little container that we cannot load all the goods.

这个集装箱很小,我们不能把所有的货物都装进去。

(六)条件状语从句

引导条件状语从句的连词主要有if、unless、as/so long as(只要)、provided (that)(条件是)、once(一旦)、in case(假使)等,条件状语从句一般主句为一般将来时,从句用一般现在时。

No discount will be allowed unless your order is over 20 tons.

除非你方订单超过20吨,否则没有折扣。

A deal will be closed as long as both parties agree to negotiate.

只要双方同意协商,生意可以达成。

(七)比较状语从句

比较状语从句一般由than、as...as、not so/as...as引导。

The goods arrived earlier than expected. 货物比预计早到达。

(八)目的状语从句

常见的连词有so that(以便于)、in order that(为了)、for fear that(以免)、in case(以免,以防)等。从句中的谓语一般与can、could、may、might、will、would、should等连用。

We will hurry shipment so that they can reach you before the selling season.

我们会加快发货,这样货物会在销售旺季前到达你处。

They prepare more stock than usual for fear that there should be a sudden surge of need.

他们准备了比往常更多的库存以防需求突然激增。

(九)让步状语从句

让步状语从句中经常使用的连词有though、although、even if(即使)、even though(即使)、much as(尽管)、as(尽管)等。

We are still unable to bring the price down even though you're our regular customer.

即使您是我们的老客户,我们仍然不能降价。

Much as we would like to cooperate with you, we find your offer unworkable.

尽管我们很想同你们合作,但我们觉得你方报价行不通。

 学习点拨

有的引导词表示的含义有两种(如since既可以表示"自从……",也可以表示"既然";while既可以表示"当……时",也可以表示"尽管";in case既可以表示"假使",也可以表示"以免,以防")或三种(如as既可以表示"当……时""因为",也可以表示"尽管"),在选择时要注意。此外,同一个含义的中文引导词有不同的

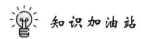

英文对应词,含义也有一些区别(如"因为""当……时"),需要在句子中把握。

函电中还有一些常见的引导词,如now that(既然)、on condition that(条件是)、lest(以免,唯恐)等需要掌握。

💡 知识加油站

"原因/结果"的几种表示方法

除了上述原因/结果状语从句以外,以下五种表示方法也可以表示"原因/结果":

◎ 动词或动词短语:cause(造成)、lead to(导致)、result in(导致)、result from(源于)、attribute... to...(把……归因于……)

◎ 介词短语:as a result of(因此)、because of(因此)、due to(因此)、owing to(因此)、on account of(由于)

◎ 副词:therefore(因此)、thus(因此)、hence(因此)

◎ 连词:so(因此)

◎ 相近表述:considering(考虑到)、in view of(鉴于)、thanks to(幸亏)

巩固与提升

[真题在线]

一、单项选择题

At present, such a growing demand for the two items can only _____ the great increase in price. (2014年第63题)

A. result from　　B. result in　　C. leads to　　D. result to

二、句子翻译

1. As our stock of these goods is limited, we would advise you to place your order as soon as possible. (2011年第93题)

2. When you get the goods ready for shipment, please let us know as soon as possible. (2012年第90题)

3. 如果价格吸引人,产品的质量又令人满意,我们会下订单。(2012年第95题写作)

4. Your price is so high that we have to purchase the goods elsewhere. (2013年第91题写作)

5. 虽然我们知道开立信用证会占压你方大量资金,但由于我们初次交易(initial/first transaction),不得不要求你方以信用证付款。(2015年第50题)

6. 由于材料柔软、耐用,我们的棉质床单销售很快。(2016年第56题写作)

[强化练习]

一、单项选择题

1. _____ there is a reduction of 3% , we won't continue our cooperation.

    A. As   B. If   C. Since   D. Unless

2. _____your L/C reached us later than scheduled, there will be a delay in shipment.

    A. Though   B. Provided   C. Once   D. Since

3. We're enclosing a list of the goods available from stock _____ you are interested.

    A. so that   B. in case   C. much as   D. even if

4. Hardly had we received your mail _____ we contacted the shipping agent.

    A. than   B. once   C. when   D. while

5. We will consider a trial order _____ you promise punctual shipment.

    A. as long as   B. even though   C. as if   D. for fear that

6. They _____ everything ready the moment they receive the down payment.

    A. get   B. will get   C. got   D. would get

7. _____ it is off-season, we still need to prepare sufficient stock for unexpected orders.

    A. Now that   B. Once   C. Even if   D. Since

8. It only involves _____ small an amount_____ we hope to make payment by T/T .

    A. such, that   B. so, that   C. such, which   D. so, as

二、句子翻译

1. Load the goods in solid wooden cases in case they should be damaged in transit.

2. Once you are interested in any product, please let us know immediately.

3. Further orders will follow on condition that the first batch satisfies our client entirely.

4. As a result of heavy commitment in the past months, we have to decline your order with regret.

5. 尽管你方订单量不是很大,我们还是会给予优惠报价。

6. 既然损失是我们粗心大意所致,我们肯定会尽快理赔。

7. 根据合同,在我们发货之前,你方应支付货款的30%。

8. 008号合同上的艺术品受损严重,无法出售了。

九、名词性从句

➤ **能力要求**

了解名词在句子中的位置及作用。

掌握主语从句、宾语从句和表语从句的基本用法。

了解同位语从句的基本用法。

➤ **知识储备**

(一)名词的位置及用法

1. 主语

This company exports silk scarfs.

2. 宾语

(1)动宾 They signed a contract.

(2)介宾 We are desirous of your response.

3. 表语

They are sales managers.

4. 同位语

(1)主语的同位语 ABC company, our regular customer, is a leading one in the line.

(2)宾语的同位语 We went to China International Imports Expo, the largest one of this year in China.

5. 宾语补足语

We name the brand happiness.

6. 定语(名词作定语一般表示事物的材料、属性、用途、范围等)

麻袋 gunny bag   销售合同 sales contract

索赔信 claim letter   交期,交货期 delivery schedule

(二)名词性从句

把原来句子中充当主语、宾语、表语或同位语的名词或名词短语换成一个句子,就构成了名词性从句。它分为四种:主语从句、宾语从句、表语从句和同位语从句。

主语从句

1. 例句

(1)That you failed to deliver the goods in time caused many problems.

你方未能及时交货造成了很多问题。

(2)It is stipulated in the contract that payment is to be effected by L/C.(it 是形式主语,that 从句为真正的主语,这样可以避免头重脚轻。)

合同规定通过信用证付款。

(3)Whether they will attend the fair is unclear.

他们是否会参加交易会尚不清楚。

2. 用法说明

(1)当陈述句充当句子主语时,引导词that不能省略。

(2)主语从句的引导词除了that以外,根据句意选择特殊疑问词when、where、how、what、whether、why等,但是要注意句子的语序为陈述句语序,即"引导词 + 主语 + 谓语动词(+ 其他成分)"。请观察下面一组句子:

Why did they choose us as a supplier remains unknown. (×)

Why they chose us as a supplier remains unknown. (√)

(3)由于主语从句通常指代一件事,所以要把握好主谓一致原则。

That you delivered the wrong goods **causes** us inconvenience.

What he said **has** secured our attention.

宾语从句

1. 例句

(1)We understand (that) you are a leading exporter of canned fruits.

我们了解到贵司是罐头水果的大出口商。

(2)They are much interested in what we displayed at the exhibition.

他们对我们在展会上展出的物品颇感兴趣。

2. 用法说明

(1)宾语从句分两种情况,一种是由及物动词引导的从句,另一种是由介词引导的从句。

(2)若宾语从句中的连词为that,that可以省略;若连词为特殊疑问词,特殊疑问词必须保留。

(3)宾语从句同主语从句一样,从句部分的语序是陈述句语序。

表语从句

1. 例句

(1)The problem is that the goods are out of stock at present. 问题是目前缺货。

(2)That's why our goods are salable. 这就是为什么我们的货物畅销。

(3)What we need is what you promised last time. 我们要的是你上次承诺的东西。

2. 用法说明

(1)在表语从句中,that不能省略。

(2)表语从句同宾语从句一样,从句部分的语序是陈述句语序,但时态不必完全一致。

(3)表语从句中表示"是否"时,使用whether,而不使用if。

The problem is **whether** they can catch the steamer this week.

(4)"It + seems/appears + that..." 构成的是表语从句,因为seem和appear是系动词,that从句充当表语。对比下面一组句子:

It seems impossible that they complete the order in one week. (主语从句,it为形式主语)

It seems that they got a large order. (表语从句,it没有实际意义,也不指代后面的that从句。若it指代从句,则seem后面缺少表语,句子结构就不完整了)

同位语从句

1. 例句

(1)The information that the market is declining troubles us.

市场正在下滑的这个消息困扰了我们。

（2）There is no doubt <u>that goods of high quality are welcomed</u>.

毫无疑问，高品质的产品受人欢迎。

（3）You have to tell us the truth <u>whether the goods were completely damaged or not</u>.

你必须告诉我们真相——货物是否完全损毁了。

2. 用法说明

（1）同位语从句的名词一般为抽象名词,主要有 news、idea、fact、promise、question、doubt、thought、hope、message、suggestion、possibility 等,后面用一个句子对抽象名词进行解释说明。

（2）同位语从句的连词以 that 居多,虽然没有实际意义,但不能省略;也可以根据句子选用 when、where、how、why、what、who、whether 等,但不使用 if。

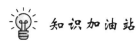 学习点拨

为了避免句子"头重脚轻"的状况,主语从句和同位语从句经常会调整句子顺序,一定程度上会影响判断。尤其是句子中出现 it 时,需要仔细分析句子结构,方能做出判断。

一个名词性从句可以只包含一个从句,也可以有两个甚至三个从句。

此外,同一意思可以使用不同的名词性从句,如:

The fact is that they will sign a contact soon.（表语从句）

That they will sign a contact soon is a fact.（主语从句）

🔅 知识加油站

同位语从句 vs 定语从句

同位语从句和定语从句隶属于不同的范畴,一般不太会混淆,但当句子中出现了抽象名词时,对于句子的理解就存在疑惑。在此,以下面的一组句子做一个简单的对比:

①The news <u>that they will reduce the price</u> reached us just now.（同位语从句）

他们要降价的消息刚刚传到。

②We got the news <u>that they sent yesterday</u>.（定语从句）

我们得到他们昨天发出的消息。

◎ 抽象名词的作用不一样

抽象名词 news 在句①的从句中没有起任何作用,而在句②的从句中充当先行词,作 sent 的宾语。

◎ 连词的作用不一样

that 在句①中起连接作用,没有意义,但是不能省略;that 在句②中是关系代词,指代 the news。由于其在从句中充当宾语成分,可以省略。

◎ 从句的作用不一样

同位语从句一般是对抽象名词进行"解释说明",使抽象意思具体化,去掉整个句子以后,句意理解可能存在困难;定语从句对抽象名词进行"修饰",去掉以后,句意会受到一定影响,但不像同位语那样那么大。

◎ 从句与抽象名词的紧密程度不一样

同位语从句一般紧跟在抽象名词后,如句①所示,但为了避免句子"头重脚轻"的状况,也可以调整如下:

The news reached us just now <u>that they will reduce the price</u>.

定语从句由于要修饰抽象名词,且抽象名词在句子中要充当成分,两者关系紧密,所以不会出现下面这种情况:

The news reached us that they sent yesterday. (×)

巩固与提升

[真题在线]

一、单项选择题

1. You were recommended to our company by the Bank of China, New York Branch, _____ told us _____ you export Chinese table cloths. (2013年第67题)

    A. that, which　　　　B. which, that　　　　C. what, that　　　　D. that, what

2. Would you please tell us _____ kind of Invoice you want, the Proforma Invoice or the Customs Invoice? (2015年第32题)

    A. this　　　　　　　B. that　　　　　　　C. what　　　　　　D. which

二、句子翻译

1. 我方相信你会同意我方产品质量上乘,价格合理。(2016年第56题)

2. Please inform us whether you agree or not. (2017年第53题)

3. It has been found that the mistake is due to one of our workers' careless packing. (2018年第51题)

4. We regret to say that they are very much inferior in quality to your sample . (2018年第53题)

5. 我们得知贵方打算购买中国纺织品。(2018年第56题)

6. 这是我们成为本领域大供应商的原因所在。(2019年第56题)

[强化练习]

一、单项选择题

1. That's _____ they chose us as their agent.

    A. because　　　　　B. whether　　　　　C. since　　　　　　D. why

2. The information came _____ the market will advance soon.

    A. that   B. how   C. when   D. if

3. Please let us know _____ you're interested or not.

    A. if   B. whether   C. which   D. that

4. Could you inform us _____ ?

    A. when will you deliver the goods   B. when will the goods be delivered

    C. when you will deliver the goods   D. when the goods will deliver

5. The problem is _____ the required goods are not available now.

    A. what   B. because   C. which   D. that

6. _____ is regrettable _____ your price doesn't match the prevailing market.

    A. It；what   B. Which；that   C. That；what   D. It；that

7. We are looking forward to _____ we need in this aspect.

    A. what   B. which   C. that   D. it

8. _____ is true is that competitive price will result in high market share.

    A. It   B. Which   C. What   D. That

二、句子翻译

1. It's understood that extra premium should be for buyer's account.

2. Please rest assured that the first batch of goods will reach you duly.

3. Our proposal is that shipment be made in four equal lots.

4. The information proves wrong that the market will advance soon.

5. 很高兴通知您货物今早平安到达我处。

6. 我们急需的是原材料和熟练的工人。

7. 信用证规定禁止转运。

8. 去何处寻找一个可靠的供应商是我们目前最大的问题。

十、虚拟语气

▶ 能力要求

掌握 if 条件句引导的虚拟语气。

掌握"should + 动词原形"表示虚拟的用法。

➤ **知识储备**

语气是一种动词形式,用来表示说话人的态度和意图。英语中有三种语气:陈述语气、祈使语气和虚拟语气。

虚拟语气表示所说的话不是事实,或者是不可能发生的情况,而是一种愿望、建议或与事实相反的假设。

(一)虚拟语气在条件从句中的应用

条件从句有两类,一是真实条件句,另一是虚拟条件句。如果假设的情况可能发生,是真实条件句,这种情况下谓语用陈述语气。如:

If time permits, we'll visit your head office next week.

如果时间允许,我们下周会参观贵司总部。

如果假设的情况是不存在的或不大可能发生的,则是虚拟条件句。如:

If you had informed us earlier, we would have covered TPND in addition to All Risks.

如果你方早点通知我们的话,我们除了投保一切险还会投保偷窃提货不着险。

if引导虚拟条件句时,主句和从句都需要用虚拟语气。具体见下表:

与何种事实相反的假设	if从句部分结构	主句结构
与现实事实相反	If + 主语 + 动词过去式 (be动词用were)	主语 + should/would/could/might +动词原形
与过去事实相反	If + 主语 + had done	主语 + should/would/could/might +have done
与将来事实相反	If + 主语+ were to + 动词原形 If + 主语+ should + 动词原形	主语 + should/would/could/might +动词原形

If I were you, I would lower the price. 如果我是你,我就会降价。

If you had packed the goods carefully, they wouldn't have been damaged.

如果你仔细包装货物的话,它们就不会被损坏了。

If I were to attend the fair tomorrow, I would get everything ready now.

如果我明天去参加展会的话,我现在会把一切准备妥当。

判断与何种事实情况相反,可以观察句子中的时间状语得知。在没有时间状语的情况下,则要借助上下文语境做出合理判断。

The sample did not arrive on time. You should have sent it earlier.

样品没有准时到达。你本应该早点发出的。

(should have done表示本应该做某事,事实上没有做;它的否定为should not have done,意为本不应该这么做,可事实上这么做了。)

(二)虚拟语气"should + do"的应用

1. 动词引导的宾语从句

一些动词引导的宾语从句时,从句部分需要使用"that + 主语 + should + do"表示虚拟语气,should可以省略。这些动词用一句话概括:一个坚持(insist),两个命令(order、command),三个建议(suggest、advise、 propose)，四个要求（ask、demand、require、request）。

We insist that the buyer（should）make payment by L/C. 我们坚持买方需用信用证付款。

They propose that shipment（should）be advanced. 他们建议提早发货。

上述动词的名词或被动形式出现时，从句部分也要使用虚拟语气。

It is our <u>requirement</u> that shipment（should）be made by one shipment.

It is <u>requested</u> that you（should）give us a firm offer.

注意：当advise意为"通知，告知"时，不需要使用虚拟语气。

※recommend和desire也适用上述结构。

2. 固定句型

结构：It's necessary/important/natural/strange/a pity + that + 主语 + should + do

It's a pity that you should not accept our price. 很可惜，你不接受我们的价格。

It's necessary that goods（should）be packed in strong materials.
货物用牢固的材料包装很有必要。

上述句型中的形容词的名词形式也需要使用虚拟语气。

It's of necessity that goods should be packed in strong materials.

（三）其他结构

除了上述两种情况外，使用虚拟语气的还有以下三种情况。

1. wish
当希望的事情不太可能发生时，需要使用虚拟语气。具体情况见下表：

与现实事实相反		动词过去式（be要用were）
与过去事实相反	主语 + wish +（that）+ 主语 +	had + 过去分词
与将来事实相反		would + 动词原形

I wish I had contacted you yesterday. 我多么希望昨天联系上您。

2. as if、as though、would rather的用法同wish一样

We would rather that we had quoted a higher price. 我们宁愿当时报一个更高的价格。

3. 固定句型：It's +（high）time that + 主语 + 动词过去式

该句型表示的意思是"该干某事了，时间已经有些晚了"。

It's time that you settled the problem. 你要来解决这个问题了。

（四）口语交际中的虚拟语气

1. 情态动词的过去式用于现在时态时，表示说话人的谦虚、客气、有礼貌、或委婉的语气，常用于日常会话中。如：

Would you be kind enough to quote us your lowest price?

2. 在一些习惯表达中。如：

You'd better start now.

学习点拨

考试中,虚拟语气通过两种形式得以体现:一种是通过时态变化(一般把时态相应地变为过去),如一般现在时变为一般过去时、一般过去时变为过去完成时、一般将来时则变为过去将来时;另一种则是针对特定动词及其变体(名词,被动语态等),使用"should + do"结构。

 知识加油站

If条件句的省略

If条件句表示虚拟语气时,if可以省略,具体变化见下表。

与事实相反	有if	省略if	变化规则
与现实事实相反	If I were you, …	Were I you, …	were提前,其余不变。*
与过去事实相反	If you had known it, …	Had you known it, …	had提前,其余不变。
与将来事实相反	If he were to do it, …	Were he to do it, …	were提前,其余不变。
	If he should do it, …	Should he do it, …	should提前,其余不变。

*注:

当if引导虚拟语气与现在事实相反且if从句部分的谓语动词不是were时,不能省略if把动词提前。

if省略,将were、had或should提前后,其实该部分已经为倒装结构。只是第一种情况把谓语动词were全部放在主语前,称之为全部倒装;后面两种情况将谓语动词的一部分(助动词had/情态动词should)提前到主语前,称之为部分倒装。

巩固与提升

[真题在线] --

句子翻译

1. If you could order over 2,000 pieces of the offered item, we would allow you a discount of 12%. (2011年第90题)

2. We advised you in our letter of Mar. 6 that we would like to place a trial order with you for 30 pieces of Flying Pigeon Bicycles. (2018年第52题)

[强化练习] ··········

一、单项选择题

1. He demanded that the meeting _____ put off.

    A. not be   B. should not   C. wouldn't   D. be not

2. _____ you require any further details of our company, please refer to Bank of China, Hangzhou.

    A. Should   B. Would   C. Could   D. Must

3. But for our good relations, we _____ that price.

    A. would not quote   B. would not have quoted

    C. couldn't quote   D. will not quote

4. It is high time that you _____.

    A. place orders   B. would place order

    C. placed orders   D. had placed order

5. _____ for the traffic jam, they should have arrived on time.

    A. Had it been   B. Had it not been

    C. It had not been   D. It not had been

6. What do you think of his proposal that we _____ design a new pattern?

    A. will   B. should   C. would   D. had

7. It is quite important that the goods _____ before shipment.

    A. must be checked   B. should check

    C. must check   D. be checked

8. They must have missed the steamer, otherwise the goods _____ then.

    A. should arrive here   B. would have arrived here

    C. has arrived here   D. arrived here

二、句子翻译

1. _____(如果你早点开立信用证的话),
we would have dispatched the goods.

2. It's proposed that _____
(关于品质的争议应当立即解决).

3. Our desire is _____
(贵司按照合同进行理赔).

4. Were you to compare our offer with others, _____
_____(你就会觉得我的价格合理).

5. But for your suggestion, _____
(交易不可能这么顺利地完成).

6. In OEM business, It's of great importance _____
_____(买方提供的商标须是合法的).

十一、it 的用法

➤ **能力要求**

掌握代词 it 的用法。

掌握引导词 it 的用法。

➤ **知识储备**

（一）代词 it

1. 指代人以外的事物。

There is a fax on the cabinet. It is from DEC Company. 柜子上有一封传真。它来自 DEC 公司。

2. 代表前面已经提到的，或将会发生的事情。

I had an negotiation with Tom. It was a complete success. 我和汤姆进行了磋商，非常成功。

4. 指时间、距离和自然现象。

It is the selling season for pineapple. 现在是菠萝的销售旺季。

It is a 3,000-mile voyage. 这是一段 3000 英里的航程。

It is stormy on the sea. 海上此时狂风暴雨。

5. 常用的固定搭配

make it 成功，及时到达　　　　believe it or not 信不信由你

（二）引导词 it

1. 引导词本身无意义，只是起一种先行引导的语法作用，在句子中作形式主语。

（1）真实主语为动词不定式

① It + be + adj. (for sb.)+ to do sth. 对于某人来说，做……是……（形容词修饰事情）

It's important for the seller to deliver the goods punctually. 对于卖方而言，准时交货非常重要。

② It + be + adj. (of sb.) + to do sth. 做……，某人……（形容词修饰人）

It is thoughtful of you to repack the goods. 把货物重新包装，你真是考虑得太周到了。

③ 固定句型

It's time to do sth. 到了做某事的时间了。

It takes/took sb. +（时间）+ to do sth. 做某事花了某人多少时间。

（2）真实主语为动名词

It is no use/bad/good doing sth. 做某事是没有用处/坏处/好处的。

（3）真实主语为主语从句

① It's + adj. + that...

It's regrettable that shipment was delayed. 很遗憾，发货延误了。

② It's + 动词过去分词 + that...

It's understood that we will bear the additional charges. 不言而喻，我们会承担额外费用。

③ It's + noun + that...

It's a pity that you didn't catch that steamer. 很遗憾,你们没能赶上那艘船。

2. 引导词本身无意义,只是起一种先行引导的语法作用,在句子中作形式宾语。

(1)真实宾语为动词不定式

The extreme weather made it impossible to make punctual shipment.

极端天气使得准时发货成为不可能。

(2)真实宾语为动名词

Our client felt it meaningless negotiating with you. 我方客人觉得同你们协商没有意义。

(3)真实宾语为宾语从句

Please see to it that the goods reach us as scheduled. 请确保货物准时到达我们这里。

3. 引导词it在强调句型中的运用

强调句型为"It is/was + 被强调部分 + that + 句子其他成分",可以强调一个句子的主语、宾语、表语及状语成分。如果被强调部分是表示人的词,也可以用who代替that。

例句:He made an apology this morning.

It's he that/who made an apology this morning. (强调he)

今天早上道歉的人是他。

It's an apology that he made this morning. (强调an apology)

他今天早上道了歉。

该句型也可以用来强调一个状语从句,如时间状语从句、地点状语从句、原因状语从句等。

It's because the goods are of high quality that they sell well.

就是因为产品品质优良他们才会畅销。

It's not until they told us that we knew the truth. 直到他们告诉我们,我们才知道真相。

※注意:

◇ 强调句型只加强语气,不改变原句的结构和意思。

◇ 强调地点或时间状语时,不要受思维定式影响而用where或when。

It is in this warehouse **where** they store raw material. (×)

It is in this warehouse **that** they store raw material. (√)

◇ 强调句型可以强调一个句子的主语、宾语、表语及状语,但是**不能强调谓语动词**。

◇ 强调句型也可以变为一般疑问句。

(陈述句) It's at this price that the goods are sold.

(一般疑问句)Is it at this price that the goods are sold?

 学习点拨

it作为常见代词之一,在函电中使用广泛。在使用时,应重点把握好三个方面的知识:第一,形式主语和宾语(尤其是固定句型)。第二,强调句型及其使用。第三,指代一件事时,把握好它和which的区别。

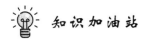 知识加油站

谓语动词的强调

对谓语动词进行强调,通常使用"do/does/did + 动词原形"这个结构,表示"真的,的确,确实……"。其中 do 有人称(第一人称、第二人称、第三人称)、时态(一般为一般现在时和一般过去时)的变化,可以是 do、does 或 did,且一般用在陈述句中。

Our client *does* appreciate your goods, but he isn't satisfied with the price.

我方客人很欣赏你方产品,但是他对价格不满意。

We *do* hope you can understand our situation now.

我们真心希望你方能理解我们现在的处境。

We *did* quote them such a price in the past.

我们以前的确给他们报过这样的价格。

巩固与提升

[真题在线]

一、单项选择题

It is after examination _____ we find the goods of high standard and are satisfied with the quality of shipment.(2018 年第 31 题)

A. as   B. which   C. what   D. that

二、句子翻译

1. We might refuse the shipment if it doesn't arrive on time.(2013 年第 93 题)

2. 请务必按合同在 9 月 30 日或之前将全部货物装运。(2015 第 56 题)

3. It has been found that the mistake is due to one of our workers' careless packing.(2018 年第 51 题)

4. We should appreciate it if you could airmail us a copy of full-range catalogue and some sample cuttings from the cloth for us to study.(2019 年第 54 题)

5. 我们确实期望在不远的将来能够与贵公司建立长期的业务关系。(2019 年第 56 题)

[强化练习] ....

一、单项选择题

1. We think _____ our duty to remind you of the establishment of L/C.

    A. that   B. it   C. this   D. what

2. We _____ purchasing your products in the past, but we couldn't persuade our clients because of your high price.

    A. do consider   B. can consider   C. did consider   D. does consider

3. We would _____ very much if you could send us a catalog covering your latest goods.

    A. appreciate it   B. obliged it   C. be appreciated   D. thank it

4. We feel _____ regrettable that the pattern required by you is out of stock.

    A. that   B. it   C. this   D. what

5. Please _____ that the L/C stipulations are in accordance with those of the S/C.

    A. see it to   B. see it clear   C. see to   D. see to it

6. Was it at this price _____ the business is done?

    A. which   B. that   C. what   D. where

7. It's because of the favorable price _____ we placed an order.

    A. which   B. why   C. what   D. that

8. It is necessary that all the goods _____ within one week.

    A. will be sent   B. would be sent   C. should be sent   D. had been better

二、句子翻译

1. 在我们的合同中,用FOB来代替CIF是不可能的。

2. 据说"永久号"昨晚已抵达上海港。

3. 我觉得在香港转运比较方便。

4. 你认为有必要坚持用FOB报价吗?

5. 我们一周前的确向他们报过价了。

6. 买方和卖方就是在这个房间讨论价格的。

7. 直到今天早上我们才把货物装上船。

8. 正是由于我们之间的良好关系,这次我们才会给予通融。

十二、省略

➤ **能力要求**

熟悉句子中省略的常见情况。

掌握复合句中的省略。

➤ **知识储备**

(一)简单句中的省略

1. 陈述句中的省略

(We're) Looking forward to your letter.

(It) Sounds interesting.

2. 疑问句中的省略

(Is there) Any problem?

(Have you) Finished packing?

3. 祈使句中的省略

(You) Kindly let us know your price.

(You) Don't break the contract.

4. 感叹句中的省略

What high quality (it is)!

5. 不定式结构的省略

(1)使役动词 let、make、have 及一部分感官动词 see、watch、notice、observe、hear 等后面作宾语补足语的不定式要省略 to,但被动时 to 要补上。

They made us (to) design a new logo.

(2)有时为了避免重复,表达相同意思的不定式符号 to 后面的内容可以省略,只保留 to。

A：Could you send me a pamphlet?　　　　B：We'd like to (send you a pamphlet).

(二)并列句中的省略

They export silk and we (export) leather shoes.

The salesperson attended the trade fair, but the sales manager didn't (attend).

(三)复合句中的省略

1. 宾语从句中的省略

(1)连接词 that 在句子中不做任何成分,可以省略。

We expect (that) you make early delivery.

(2)从句中的主语与主句中主语一致,且当从句由"wh-"开头的疑问词引导一个句子时,从句可以省略为"wh- + to do"结构。

We don't know where to import the material.

2. 定语从句中的省略

(1)在限制性定语从句中,可省略作宾语的关系代词 whom、which、that。

We need a person（whom）we can trust as our exclusive agent.

Please send us a catalog covering the goods（which）we are interested in.

(2)在限制性定语从句中,当先行词在从句中作主语且谓语动词为 be 动词时,可以省略"which/that/who + be"。

The ship（which/that is）due to sail for Shanghai tomorrow is called "Victory".

You can contact Mr. Smith（who is）in charge of the department.

（四）状语从句中的省略

1. 时间状语从句省略

While（you are）quoting, please state the delivery schedule.

Please contact us when（it is）available.

2. 条件状语从句省略

We won't make any change unless（we are）instructed.

Once（they are）equipped, they will help you save time and money.

3. 方式状语从句省略

As（we are）requested, we are now sending you an offer.

4. 比较状语从句省略

The price today is higher than（it was）yesterday.

（五）特殊情况

1. 在某些动词后含有宾语补语或主语补语的复合结构中省略 to be 的情况

We consider our business（to be）mutually beneficial.

2. 句意比较明确时,可省略相同部分

If one of the original policy has been accomplished, the others（are）to be void.

3. 口语交际习惯的省略

We shall do everything（that）we can（do）to help you.

📖 学习点拨

句子的省略是建立在约定俗成的基础上。省略的通常是句子中原有的或相同的部分,不太会影响意思的传递。**主语的省略、主语和谓语一同省略**的情况比较常见。

商函交际中不但会有句子省略的情况,也会使用一些固定的缩写短语用于交流,如 ASAP（as soon as possible）、MOQ（minimum order quantity）。

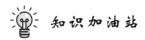 知识加油站

in 在句子中的省略

They <u>have trouble/difficulty (in)</u> finding a reliable supplier.

He <u>spent a lot of time (in)</u> designing the new logo.

We <u>are busy (in)</u> loading the goods.

We <u>succeeded (in)</u> sending the goods in spite of the bad weather.

They <u>lack experience (in)</u> sourcing new clients.

She packed the goods <u>(in) the same way</u> as others did.

巩固与提升

[真题在线]

句子翻译

1. 如感兴趣,敬请联系我们。(2014年第95题)

2. 很高兴收到你方4月10日的询价。(2016年第56题)

3. 早盼为复。(2016年第56题)

4. 唛头:由卖方设计。(2017年第56题)

[强化练习]

一、单项选择题

1. We are sending you the samples _____ requested.

    A. be   B. are   C. as   D. at

2. The ship _____ tomorrow is Princess.

    A. due to sail   B. is due to sail

    C. due to sailing   D. which is due to sailing

3. We may consider appointing an agent in that area _____ necessary.

    A. where   B. as   C. while   D. if

4. Everything goes smoothly as _____.

    A. plans   B. planning   C. planned   D. plan

5. Don't enter the warehouse unless _____.

    A. you ask   B. you are asked   C. you asked   D. you are asked to

6. We believe the initial business will prove _____ for both parties.

    A. benefit   B. beneficial   C. beneficially   D. benefits

7. Unless otherwise _____, we will cover the goods as usual.

    A. instruction   B. instructing   C. instructed   D. instruct

8. The arrival of goods is later than _____.

    A. expect   B. expects   C. expecting   D. expected

二、句子翻译

1. 运输：不晚于7月21日。

2. 现附寄一份电子目录。

3. 清点数量时，请一定要仔细。

4. 如果有必要的话，我们会联系船公司。

5. Concerning our credit, please direct all your inquiries to our banker, Bank of Ningbo.

6. Our products, made of fine material, enjoy fast sales in east European countries.

7. While examining the goods, we noticed some of them damaged.

8. They won't take part in the fair though invited.

商函写作篇

一、信函格式

➤ **能力要求**

了解外贸商函的三种书写格式。

掌握商函信件各部分的写作规范。

理解商务写作的礼貌原则。

➤ **知识储备**

1. 信函格式

商务信函的格式主要包括以下三种：

齐头式（Blocked Style）	缩进式（Indented Style）	混合式（Modified Style）
信头	信头	信头
日期	日期	日期
封内名称及地址	封内名称及地址	封内名称及地址
称呼	称呼	称呼
标题	标题	标题
正文	正文	正文
结尾敬语	结尾敬语	结尾敬语
签名	签名	签名
附件	附件	附件

必要构成部分：信头、日期、封内名称及地址、正文和结尾敬语。

特殊构成部分：编号、交由、标题、附件和经办记号。

2. 各部分书写规范

（1）日期

Feb. 10, 2020（英式）　　　　10 Feb., 2020（美式）

（2）称呼

①Dear Sirs,（两个单词都大写首字母,后接逗号,译为"敬启者"）

②Dear Sir/Madam,

③Dear Mr. /Mrs./Ms. + 姓（有明确收件人时,一般使用该格式）

（3）标题

标题能使收信人对信件的主要内容一目了然。标题前常有Re字样，后接冒号，意为"事由"，加下划线以显醒目。

事由：2000套AC05洗衣机　　　　Re：2000 Sets of Washing Machines Art. No.AC05

（4）结尾敬语

Yours faithfully，/ Yours sincerely,（注意Yours中的y要大写，faithfully/sincerely的第一个字母小写，且以逗号结尾，译为"敬上，谨启"。）

（5）附件

提示随函附寄的资料，如正文中明确提及附寄（enclose or attach）某物时，最后部分用enclosure或encl.引导，如：

Enclosure：E-catalogue　　　　Encl.：Sales Contract DE05

3. 正文书写原则

（1）所给的英文参考词必须全部使用，不要用自己组织的语言来代替所给的参考单词。

（2）段落清晰，严格按照中文提示要求，一般以三个段落或四个段落为主。

（3）尽量利用商函固定套语或习惯表达来贯穿全文，体现专业英语的规范和特质。

 学习点拨

考试中对商函格式的考查主要侧重两个方面：一是以何种格式书写，若没有特殊规定，则可以自由选择。二是各部分规范要求，尤其是称呼、标题、正文的段落、结尾敬语四个部分，大小写和书写是否规范。

 知识加油站

信封格式的书写

DHE Trading Co.

P. O. Box 2257（发信人地址）

Amsterdam，Netherlands

Sangle Trading Corporation

Rm 208-220 Jingwei Bldg

Ningbo Zhejiang China

315012（收信人地址）

巩固与提升

[真题在线]

Write an English Business Letter of **indented style** containing 150-200 words, Chinese hints given below：(2017年第56题)

Chinese hints(中文提示)：

敬启者：

感谢贵方3月30日的报价函和样品,我方发现价格和品质都达到我们的预期。我们很高兴按照下列条款和条件下订单：

商品名称：女士唐装

面料：100% 真丝

数量：10000件,5% 溢短装由卖方选定

单价：每件98欧元,成本加运费保险费到德国汉堡

总金额：98万欧元

包装：每箱装100件

装运期限：不迟于2016年5月30日

装运港：中国宁波

目的港：德国汉堡

唛头：由卖方设计

付款方式：100% 不可撤销即期信用证付款,在2016年5月10日之前开到卖方,该信用证在装运日期后15天内在中国议付有效

我们期待贵方确认订单。

谨启

[强化练习]

1. Write an English Business Letter of **blocked style** containing about 100 words, using the reference words and the Chinese hints below:

Reference words: manufacturer, leading, superior to, exceed

Chinese hints(中文提示):

敬启者:

很高兴收到你方的询价函。

现来函告知,我们是中国最大的电扇厂家之一,已有58年的业务经验。我们的产品以其质量优良、交货迅速而名闻遐迩,其质量和价格均优于其他产品。

随函附寄最新的带有价目表的目录和样本。如果你方订单超过2000台,我们愿给予10%的折扣。我们确信你方会发现我方产品是货真价实的。

盼早复。

敬上

_____

_____

_____

_____

_____

_____

_____

_____

_____

_____

_____

2. Write an English Business Letter of **modified style** containing about 120 words, using the reference words and the Chinese hints below:

Reference words: on a reasonable level, to be frank, on the rise, be prepared to do

Chinese hints(中文提示):

敬启者:

<u>货号258的男式衬衫</u>

你方6月18日来信收到,谢谢。

我们的全棉男士衬衫定价合理,很难给你们任何折扣。关于此报价,你们可以向其他供应商咨询。坦诚地说,我们已经给予了最优惠的报价。此外,原材料的价格一直在上涨,希望你们能理解我们的处境。鉴于我们过去友好的合作关系,我们愿意给予3%的数量折扣。

盼望贵方慎重考虑我们的建议,并请尽早传真予以确认。

敬上

_____

_____

_____

_____

_____

_____

_____

_____

_____

_____

二、句子翻译

➤ 能力要求

了解商函写作中句子翻译策略。

熟悉常见的句子翻译错误类型。

掌握句子翻译中逗号的处理技巧。

➤ 知识储备

(一)句子翻译策略

翻译时,首先确定句子的主干部分(主语和谓语)和次要部分(宾语、定语、状语、补语等),构建起句子的基本框架。

其次,把握好时态和语态。通过句中的时间状语或时间状语从句,落实好时态。如果缺少时间状语,则需要综合考虑句子的语境,把握上下文,有时还需要展开合理的逻辑思考,方能确定句子时态。句子的语态通常以主动语态居多,但有时为了突出宾语,或不需要说明主语时,就需要使用被动语态。

最后,注意单词拼写和标点符号等细节。

(二)句子翻译中常见语法错误

单句翻译中的错误

1. 谓语动词重复或缺失

(1)谓语be动词和实义动词重叠

① 他们还是想采购我们的产品。

They are still want to purchase our goods. (×)

They still **want** to purchase our goods. (√)

(本句的谓语动词是"想要",去掉are。)

② 你方价格与市场不符合。

Your price isn't match the market level. (×)

Your price **doesn't match** the market level. (√)

Your price **isn't in line with** the market level. (√)

(本句的谓语是"不符合",把 is 改为 does,或把 match 改为 in line with。)

(2)谓语缺失(尤其是介词短语包含动词含义时)

① 请确保信用证条款与合同条款相一致。

Please make sure that the terms in the L/C in exact accordance with those in contract. (×)

Please make sure that the terms in the L/C **are** in exact accordance with those in contract. (√)

(in exact accordance with 是介词短语,不是谓语,需在它前面加 are。)

② 我们已收到你方的邮件。

We in receipt of your e-mail. (×)

We **are** in receipt of your e-mail. (√)

(in receipt of 意为"收到",是介词短语,需加 be 作谓语。)

2. 冠词使用有误

(1)冠词多余

① We believe our offer is in the line with the market. (×)

(in line with 为固定短语,表示"与……一致",去掉 the。)

② The goods needed are out of the stock. (×)

(out of stock 为固定短语,表示"缺货",去掉 the。)

(2)冠词缺失

① In event of loss or damage, you should contact the survey agent immediately. (×)

(in the event of 为固定短语,表示"假如",加 the。)

② With view to promoting the sales, we will allow special discount this time. (×)

(with a view to 为固定短语,表示"为了",加 a。)

3. 词性混淆

(1)名词与动词混淆

① 我们会尽快发货。

We will prompt shipment. (×)

We will **make/effect** prompt shipment. (√)

(prompt shipment 是名词短语,will 后要用动词原形,添加 make 或 effect。)

② 请注意报价有效期为 10 天。

Please attention that our offer remains valid for 10 days. (×)

Please **note** that our offer remains valid for 10 days. (√)

(attention 是名词,please 后面要用动词原形,把它改为 note。)

(2)名词与形容词混淆

① 我们很高兴收到你方来函。

We are pleasure to receive your letter. (×)

We are **pleased** to receive your letter. (√)

（pleasure 是名词，pleased 是形容词，作 be 的表语，表示 we 的状态。）

② 破损是由于我们工人的粗心大意造成的。

The breakage was due to the careless of our workers. （×）

The breakage was due to the **carelessness** of our workers. （√）

（careless 是形容词，本句中的粗心大意是名词，应该是 carelessness。）

（3）实意动词与系动词混淆

① 我们的报盘有效期为 10 天。

Our offer remains validly for 10 days only. （×）

Our offer remains **valid** for 10 days only. （√）

（remain 是系动词，后接 valid，表示报价的有效性。）

② 你们的价格看起来不能接受。

Your price seems unacceptably. （×）

Your price seems **unacceptable**. （√）

（seem 是系动词，后接 unacceptable，构成系表结构。）

（4）形容词与副词混淆

① 这个价格会帮你们站稳市场。

This price will help you stand firm in the market. （×）

This price will help you stand **firmly** in the market. （√）

（firm 是形容词，不能放在动词 stand 后作状语，把它改为副词。）

② 我们的产品在贵地越来越受欢迎。

Our goods are increasing popular at your end. （×）

Our goods are **increasingly** popular at your end. （√）

（increasingly 是副词，修饰 popular，不放在 be 动词后作表语。）

（5）副词与连词混淆

① 原材料价格一直在上涨，因此我们不得不调价。

The price of raw material is on the rise, therefore we have to adjust the price. （×）

The price of raw material is on the rise. **Therefore**, we have to adjust the price. （√）

（therefore 是副词，不是连词，不能用来连接两个句子。）

（6）状语过长，误将其看成一个句子。

① 为了使你方对我们的产品有一个大致的印象，我们现寄一份目录。

In order to let you have a general idea of our products. We're sending you a catalog. （×）

In order to let you have a general idea of our products, **we**'re sending you a catalog. （√）

We're sending you a catalog in order **that** you can have a general idea of our products. （√）

（in order to 引导目的状语，是一个短语，不能加句号；也可以把它改为 in order that。）

4. 动词搭配不当

① 早日开证可以使我们能够早日发货。

Earlier establishment of L/C will make us to dispatch the goods earlier. （×）

Earlier establishment of L/C will **make** us dispatch the goods earlier. （√）

Earlier establishment of L/C will **enable** us to dispatch the goods earlier. （√）

(make 和 enable 都有"使……能够"的意思,但搭配结构不同:make 通常使用 make sb. do sth. 结构,而 enable 使用 enable sb. to do sth.。)

② 他们不会冒险大量采购。

They won't risk to buy in large quantities. (×)

They won't risk **buying** in large quantities. (√)

(risk 作动词时,后接名词或动名词短语。)

5. 主谓不一致

(1)当含有介词的名词短语充当主语时,主语辨别不清

① 这种款式的商品很畅销。

Goods of this style sells well. (×)

Goods of this style **sell** well. (√)

(goods of this style 的中心词是 goods,所以谓语动词用 sell。)

② 非常感谢你方对我方产品的及时关注。

Your prompt attention to our goods were highly appreciated. (×)

Your prompt attention to our goods **was** highly appreciated. (√)

(your prompt attention to our goods 的中心词是 attention,是不可数名词,所以用 was。)

(2)主语单数原则混淆

① 就赔偿而言,5000 美元是一个大数目。

5,000 dollars were a big sum in terms of compensation. (×)

5,000 dollars **was** a big sum in terms of compensation. (√)

② 我们的客人户想要的是你们对延误的解释。

What our clients want are your explanation for the delay. (×)

What our clients want **is** your explanation for the delay. (√)

归纳:表示时间、距离、价格、度量等的名词充当主语,谓语动词通常要用单数形式;由不定式短语、动名词短语或主语从句充当主语时,谓语动词通常要用单数形式。

(3)就近原则和就远原则混淆

① 不但老客户们对新款式感兴趣,新客户也对它感兴趣。

Not only regular customers but also the new client show their interest in the new model. (×)

Not only regular customers but also the new client **shows** their interest in the new model. (√)

Both regular customers and the new client **show** their interest in the new model. (√)

② 最新的价目表连同几件样品昨天已经寄出。

The latest price list together with several samples were sent yesterday. (×)

The latest price list together with several samples **was** sent yesterday. (√)

归纳:由 or、either...or...、neither...nor...、not only...but also... 等连接的并列主语,谓语动词与最靠近它的主语保持一致;由 with、together with、as well as、in addition to、rather than、including、as much as 等连接的并列主语,谓语动词与离它较远的主语保持一致。

从句翻译中的错误

1. 连词缺失

① 我们是你们的老客户,能否给予特别的折扣?

We are your regular customer, could you allow us a special discount? (×)

Since/As we are your regular customer, could you allow us a special discount? (√)

归纳:两个单句连接必须要有一个连词。

2. 连词重叠

① 尽管你们的颜色吸引人,但是价格没有竞争力。

Though your color is attractive, but the offer is not competitive. (×)

Though your color is attractive, the offer is not competitive. (√)

Your pattern is attractive, **but** the offer is not competitive. (√)

(though 和 but 都是连词,去掉其中一个即可。)

② 因为目前市场下跌,所以我们无法接受报价。

As the market is declining at present, so we're unable to accept your offer. (×)

As the market is declining at present, we're unable to accept your offer. (√)

The market is declining at present, **so** we're unable to accept your offer. (√)

(as 和 so 都是连词,去掉其中一个即可。)

其他错误

1. 最高级前的修饰词重叠

① 这是我们今年的最新款。

This is our the latest style this year. (×)

This is our/the latest style this year. (√)

(物主代词 our 和冠词 the 功能重叠,两者选其一皆可。)

2. 时间状语或地点状语前出现介词,导致重复

① 他们这个月会发货。

They will send the goods in this month. (×)

They will send the goods this month. (√)

(this month 是时间状语,去掉 in。)

归纳:last/this/next + 时间,本身就是状语,前面不需要介词。

② 订购的产品会准时到达那儿。

The ordered goods will get to there on time. (×)

The ordered goods will get there on time. (√)

(there 是副词,作地点状语,前面不需要介词。)

3. 主谓搭配不当

① 我们现在缺货。

We are out of stock now. (×)

Goods are out of stock. (√)

(out of stock 的主语是货不是人。)

4. 货号、编号等位于主体之前

① 客户对货号258的产品颇感兴趣。

Clients are much interested in Item No.28 goods. (×)

Clients are much interested in goods Item No.28. (√)

归纳:货号、编号等应当位于主体之后,且不需要of。

5. 动词短语结构混淆

① 他曾向我们保证准时交货。

He assured us punctual shipment. (×)

He assured us **of** punctual shipment. (√)

[assure sb. of sth. 是固定搭配,使用"v. + sb. + of sth." 结构的动词还有 remind/inform/advise(通知)/convince(使某人信服)]。

6. 望文生义,用词在语境中不当

(1)名词意思相近,使用不当

① 他是我们的长期合作伙伴。

He is our long-time partner. (×)

He is our **long-term** partner. (√)

(time表示"期限、期",term表示"期间",long-term是固定短语。)

(2)动词意思相近,使用不当

① 本地信息表明市场即将上涨。

The information states that the market will advance soon. (×)

The information **shows** that the market will advance soon. (√)

[state 和 show 都有"表明,说明"的意思。state 是正式用语,表示"(向某人)陈述(意见、立场等)";show 表示"表明",结合语境,show更贴切。]

(3)形容词意思相近,使用不当

① 他们给我们下了一个大订单。

They placed a big order with us. (×)

They placed a **large/substantial** order. (√)

② 我们已经遭受了巨大的损失。

We have sustained big loss. (×)

We have sustained **huge/considerable** loss. (√)

[big指代人的个头、体型之大;large指代事物的宽幅、体量之大;substantial指代(数量、程度等)相当的、显著的;huge指代大型事物的结构,或数量之庞大、巨大;considerable指代(数量、程度等)可观的、相当大的。]

(4)副词意思相近,使用不当

① 请将装运日期和信用证有效期分别延展至6月15日和6月30日。

Please extend shipment date and validity of L/C to June 15 and June 30 separately. (×)

Please extend shipment date and validity of L/C to June 15 and June 30 **respectively**. (√)

(separately是副词,意为"分别地,分离地",侧重将物体或事情分成两部分;respectively意为"分别地",重点强调一一对应。)

句子中译英时,逗号的处理

1. 当逗号前是状语时,逗号一般不发生变化

① 目前,他们很忙。(时间状语)

At present, they're quite busy.

② 为了赶上这班船,我们上周加了班。(目的状语)

To catch this steamer, we worked overtime last week.

2. 当逗号前是表达情感的状语时,可以按上述情形处理,也可以将句子合并构成宾语从句,用 that 来代替逗号

① 很遗憾,我们不能提前发货。

Much to our regret, we cannot advance shipment.(处理成状语)

We regret **that** we cannot advance shipment.(合并为宾语从句)

② 很高兴,你们对我们的产品感兴趣。

To our pleasure, you're interested in our products.(处理成状语)

We are pleased **that** you're interested in our products.(合并为宾语从句)

3. 当逗号前后都是句子且没有连词时,将逗号变成句号;也可根据句意,变为复合句或并列句,逗号不变

① 这是我们的最低价,我们不会再降价了。

This is our lowest offer. **We** won't make further reduction.(逗号变句号)

Since this is our lowest offer, we won't make further reduction.(构建原因状语从句)

② 这是样品,它会帮你更好地了解我们的产品。

This is our sample. **It** will help you know better about our products.(逗号变成句号)

This is our sample **and** it will help you know better about our products.(改为并列句)

This is our sample, **which** will help you know better about our products.(构建定语从句)

4. 将逗号和后面合并,变为介词短语构成的状语

① 我们已经开立了即期信用证,金额为20000美元。

We have established a sight L/C **for** the amount of 20,000 dollars.

② 请给我们报FOB宁波价,7月发货。

Please quote us on FOB Ningbo basis **with** shipment in July.

③ 兹自我介绍,我们是一家服装公司。

We introduce ourselves **as** a garment company.

 学习点拨

句子中译英需要在以下几个方面做出努力:一是夯实基础,掌握必备的字词、短语及固定句型;二是梳理语法知识,句子的正确翻译需要语法作为支撑;三是把握细节,单词拼写、同义词或近义词的选用、标点符号的处理,以及文字的转化等都会影响句子翻译的准确度。

"有"在翻译中的处理

◎ 某人/某物拥有(have)

They have trade partners worldwide. (他们在世界各地都有贸易伙伴。)

The company has a working staff of 200. (公司有200名员工。)

◎ 某地、某处有某物(there be句型)

There is keen competition in the EU market. (欧盟市场竞争激励。)

There are only 20 tons in the warehouse. (仓库只有20吨了。)

◎ 事物拥有某种特点(enjoy)

Our goods enjoy high popularity. (我们的产品很畅销。)

They enjoy a high reputation all over the world. (他们在国内外都享有盛誉。)

◎ 产品具备某种特质(be of... 结构)

Our goods are of exquisite designs. (我们的产品设计精美。)

◎ 表示所属(own)

It's a stated-owned company. (这是一家国有企业。)

巩固与提升

[真题在线]

句子翻译

1. 本公司皮革产品在国内外市场享有盛誉。(2011年写作)

2. 我们有兴趣购买货号为MS1201的男士衬衣。(2012年写作)

3. 你方5月5日的电子邮件已收到,谢谢。(2013年写作)

4. 市场上需求量很大。(2014年写作)

5. 由于双方共同努力,因此能如此顺利地达成交易。(2015年写作)

6. 此低报价使我方获利甚微。(2019年写作)

[强化练习]

一、句子翻译

1. 样品将另邮。

2. 很抱歉,我们不能接受贵司的还盘。

3. 我们坚信我们的产品货真价实。

4. 全套目录连同所需的样品今早已寄出。

5. 如果第一笔订单得以顺利执行,我们会考虑续订 2000 罐。

6. 我们急需订购的货物,请尽快发货。

7. DC005 信用证以 DBC 公司为受益人。

8. 因为原材料短缺,所以产品价格剧烈上涨。

二、改错(找出句子的一处错误并改正)

1. Goods No.25 in the catalog is of interest to us.　　　　(　)　_____
　　　A　　　　　　B　C　　D

2. If your order over 2000 packets, we will allow a 3% discount.　(　)　_____
　A　　　　　B　　　C　　　D

3. Please note that our offer remains validity only in May.　　(　)　_____
　　　　　A　　　　　B　　　C　　　D

4. Though our price is slightly higher, they still like to purchase this goods.　(　)　_____
　　A　　　　　　B　　　　　　　　C　　D

5. We shall be appreciate it if you can meet our request for earlier delivery.　(　)　_____
　　　　　A　　　B　　　　　C　　　　　D

6. Much as we would like to trade with you, but we find your price unacceptable.　(　)　_____
　　A　　　　　　　　　　B　　C　　　　　　　D

参考文献

[1] 祝卫,程洁,谈英.国际贸易操作能力实用教程[M].上海:上海人民出版社,2006.

[2] 吴百福.进出口贸易实务教程[M].上海:上海人民出版社,2003.

[3] 闫兴伯,黄宪西.商务英语函电[M].北京:高等教育出版社,2012.

[4] 徐宝良.外贸商函[M].北京:高等教育出版社,2012.

[5] 李辉,徐佩文.外贸英文函电习题册[M].北京:对外经济贸易大学出版社,2015.

[6] 余世民.国际货运代理基础理论与实务[M].广州:暨南大学出版社,2010.

[7] 于丽娟.外贸商函[M].北京:高等教育出版社,2019.

[8] 王占九,李俊香.高职高专实用英语语法[M].苏州:苏州大学出版社,2008.

单词篇

一、单词拼写

[真题在线]

一、词语互译

1. sales contract   2. 检验机构   3. 商业合同   4. contract

5. 保单   6. insurance amount   7. 装船通知   8. insurance application

9. 资信状况;财务状况   10. 承约过多;履约过多

二、句子翻译

1. Please extend the shipment date and validity of L/C to July 5 and July 20 respectively.

2. 我方期待得到(你方)对这次延误的解释。

3. 感谢贵司的合作,期待收到进一步的订单。

4. The L/C in your favor stipulated in the contract has been established/opened through Bank of China, Ningbo.

5. 在没有得到你方明确/具体的保险要求情况下,我们已经为订购的货物按照发票金额的110%投保了水渍险。

6. We assure you of prompt shipment.

[强化练习]

一、词语互译

1. illustrated catalogue   2. specific enquiry   3. export license

4. trial order   5. financial status   6. labor cost

7. without delay   8. shipping instructions

二、选词填空

1. abroad   2. insure   3. raise   4. special

5. intend   6. contract   7. exception   8. accommodate

三、单项选择题

1. C   2. A   3. B   4. C   5. C   6. B   7. A   8. C

四、句子翻译

1. Samples will be sent under separate cover.

2. If there is any problem，please don't hesitate to contact us.

3. Haier（Brand）electric appliances are quite salable both at home and abroad.

4. Our latest offer will remain valid within ten days.

5. We assure you that the goods will reach the port of destination punctually. /We assure you of punctual arrival of our goods at the port of destination.

6. As for payment，we regret our inability to meet your request at present.

7. Please open an L/C in our favor through a bank acceptable to us.

8. It's regrettable that we have to raise the price by 5%.

二、重点动词及拓展

[真题在线]

一、单项选择题

1. C 2. A 3. A 4. D 5. C 6. B

二、句子翻译

1. We will meet/satisfy your request at the most competitive prices.

2. 感谢贵司的合作,期待收到进一步的订单。

3. You're quite satisfied with our offer.

4. We trust that you will be satisfied with the trial order this time.

5. 我方决定向你方做出让步,按照你方的要求给出更低的价格/降低价格。

6. 我们建议货物分两批等量装运。请告知你方同意与否。

7. 我方已经收到我们从你处订购的货物,但遗憾地说,这些产品的品质比样品品质低劣得多。

8. If you're interested in any item listed in the catalog，please let us have your specific inquiry.

[强化练习]

一、选词填空

1. regrettable   2. satisfied   3. acceptable   4. competitiveness

5. reach   6. your sending   7. agreeable   8. assured

二、用所给词的正确形式填空

1. interest   2. agreement   3. confirmed   4. coverage

5. appreciated   6. competition   7. informed   8. regrettable

三、句子翻译

1. Please inform us of the shipping date/date of shipment.

2. We regret to have caused you so much inconvenience.

3. We're quite satisfied with goods Item No.008.

4. 我方很满意贵司的上一批货物,决定续订。

5. 尽管我方很认可你们产品的品质,但是不能同意你方的报价。

6. 我方认为,考虑到本地市场竞争激烈,降价会对贵司有利。

三、普通英语VS专业术语

[真题在线]••

短语或句子翻译

1. 实盘

2. valid for negotiation in China

3. 如果贵司能订购所报价货物2000件以上,我们会给予12%的折扣。

4. 在绝大多数情况下,我们的支付惯例是保兑的不可撤销的即期信用证。

5. trade negotiation

6. 主动报盘

7. 我方想要就相同产品向贵司下一个复订单。

8. general average

[强化练习]••

一、词语互译

1. 完税后交货   2. 远期汇票   3. 分两批等量(运输)   4. 运费成本

5. non-firm offer   6. general practice   7. subject/captioned goods   8. market share

二、句子翻译

1. 贵司报价与市场行情不符。

2. 双方在价格上已经达成一致。

3. 通过ABC公司的介绍,我方获悉贵司是服装的大出口商。

4. 若贵司能降价5%,我们也许可以成交。

5. We learn your name from the 2019 China International Import Expo.

6. In order to cover the rising costs, we have to raise the price by 5%.

7. The extra premium should be for buyer's account.

8. We're much interested in goods Type No.228.

三、改错(找出句子中的一处错误并改正)

1. usually → usual   2. with → for   3. at → to/by   4. equally → equal

5. covering → to cover   6. at → to   7. issuing → issued   8. confirmed → confirming

词缀篇

[真题在线]••

一、单项选择题

1. D

二、短语或句子翻译

1. 信用证的修改

2. 保险由卖家办理,按发票金额的110%投保水渍险和碰撞破碎险。

3. 我们希望贵司能在本月底前开立相关的信用证。

4. 财务状况

5. 付款行

[强化练习]

一、根据要求进行词性变化

1. 将下列动词变成其相应名词

① extension   ② enquiry   ③ requirement   ④ proposal

⑤ conveyance   ⑥ breakage   ⑦ packing   ⑧ satisfaction

2. 将下列词变成其反义词

① regardless   ② irrevocable   ③ disagreement   ④ misunderstanding

⑤ unstable   ⑥ non-transferable   ⑦ irregular   ⑧ incapable

二、用所给词的正确形式填空

1. validity   2. acceptable   3. inconvenience   4. apology

5. inability   6. informed   7. promotion   8. priority

三、句子翻译

1. 我方期待贵司早日确认我方订单。

2. 下面提及的货物可供现货。

3. 请注意我方的最小订单/最低起订量为5000码。

4. 由于承约过多,我方目前不能接受贵司订单。

5. 请重新考虑我们修订过的价格,并期待你方早日同意。

6. 在国际贸易中,一笔交易的达成通常需要经历多轮磋商。

7. (买卖)双方最终达成一致,合同生效。

8. 请在规定的时间内交货,以便我们赶上销售旺季。

词组篇

一、同义、近义词汇总

[真题在线]

一、翻译句子

1. We're very interested in your goods, so please quote us the lowest price for 600 metric tons of following goods.

2. We will place a trial order with you, if you can allow us a 5% discount.

3. We would be grateful if you can make shipment at an early date/as soon as possible.

4. We regret to say that we are unable to/it's impossible for us to make further reduction in price as there is little profit for such goods now.

5. If the quantity ordered of every style is not less than 1000 yards, we can give/allow you a 2% discount.

6. We take this opportunity to establish business relations with you.

[强化练习]

一、单项选择题

1. C 2. B 3. B 4. A 5. D 6. C 7. B 8. D

二、用所给词的正确形式填空

1. to allow	2. receiving	3. closing	4. (should) be made
5. to do	6. to satisfy	7. popularity	8. Referring

三、句子翻译

1. Please ensure/see to it that the stipulations of L/C are in exact accordance with those in contract.

2. Would you please furnish us with some samples for our reference?

3. It is understood that extra premium shall be at our expense.

4. The first batch of the goods are to be delivered in June and the remainder in July.

5. Having been in the line of home electric appliance for more than 30 years, we establish good relationship with clients at home and abroad.

6. Please do your utmost to have the L/C established so that we can effect shipment at an early date.

7. Catalog as well as the latest pricelist will be sent under separate cover.

二、外贸商函术语大分类 & 三、专业术语大集合

[真题在线]

词语互译

1. T/T (telegraphic transfer)　　　　　2. shipping advice

3. proforma invoice　　　　　4. insurance premium

5. consignee　　　　　6. 装船通知

7. reciprocal L/C　　　　　8. duplicate order

9. 担保提货

[强化练习]

一、词语互译

1. type sample　　　　　2. gross for net

3. notify party　　　　　4. specific enquiry

5. container yard　　　　　6. minimum order/minimum order quantity

7. 不可抗力　　　　　8. 注册资本

9. 重量单　　　　　10. 商船

11. 海关发票　　　　　12. 出口许可证

二、句子翻译

1. 我们会通过电汇方式将全部的金额汇付给您。

2. 这种风险可以投保,费率为0.7%。

3. 假如(货物)有损失或损坏,应立即与承保人联系。

4. 各种成本的持续上涨迫使制造商相应地调整价格。

5. 出口商希望(进口商)提前付款,而进口商则希望赊账。

6. 损失由你方包装不当造成,(金额)达2500美元。

7. 数量:30000码,可增减5%,由卖方决定。

8. 如有质量争议,必须提交检验报告作为证据。

常用句子篇

[真题在线]

句子翻译

1. We regret that your price is too high to be acceptable.

2. We understand your difficult situation, but we regret we cannot consider your request for payment by D/A (Documents against Acceptance).

3. 我们再次就我们的错误向你们致歉,这肯定给你们带来了诸多不便。

4. 承蒙贵国马克先生的推荐,我方得知贵方是电子产品的主要进口商之一,并且愿与我方建立业务关系。

5. 鉴于你方的良好声誉,我们破例接受凭单付现的付款方式。

[强化练习]

句子翻译

1. We take this opportunity to establish business relations with you.

2. The price of raw material has been on the rise recently. Such being the case, we have to adjust our offer.

3. Goods Type No. AC05 are out of stock and we recommend Type AC04 as a substitute.

4. We are in receipt of your letter requesting us to advance shipment. At present, we can deliver only 50 M/Ts.

5. 尽管我们很认可你们的品质,但是很遗憾,你们的价格与现行价格不符。

6. 接受你们目前的报价意味着没有任何利润。能否考虑适度降价?

7. 货物已经备妥待运。能否加速开立信用证?

8. 对于货物的损坏,我方向你方表示歉意,并向你方保证我方定会及时处理你方的索赔。

语法篇

一、形容词和形容词的比较等级

[真题在线]

一、单项选择题

C

二、句子翻译

1. 在中国香港装运能使货物早日送达贵方,因为中国香港开往美国的船舶非常频繁。

2. 我们已经收到订购的产品,但是很遗憾,这些产品比贵方的样品质量低劣得多。因此,我方要求贵方降价30%。

3. 由于信用证上规定的装船日期是4月30日,而且不能再延长,因此货物必须不迟于上述日期装船。

[强化练习]

一、用所给词的正确形式填空

1. latest	2. more	3. more competitive	4. the most popular
5. broader	6. those	7. further	8. worse

二、短语翻译

1. 尽早/在您方便时尽早	2. 最小订单	3. 外包装
4. 底价	5. inner packing	6. more or less clause
7. the maximum concession	8. most-favored-nation treatment	

三、句子翻译

1. 贵司可以联系我们获取更多的产品细节。

2. 我方将邮寄样品以供你方进一步考虑。

3. 由于市场上的激烈竞争,利润变得越来越微薄。

4. 请尽快/不耽搁发货。

5. We shall much appreciate it if you can give priority to our request.

6. Price from your competitor is 5% lower than yours.

7. Earlier establishment of L/C will ensure earlier shipment.

8. For exporters, payment in advance by clients is ideal/ the ideal one.

二、介 词

[真题在线]

单项选择题

1. C 2. C 3. A 4. C 5. D 6. B 7. C 8. C 9. C 10. C

[强化练习]

一、单项选择题

1. C　2. C　3. D　4. B　5. A　6. C　7. A　8. D　9. C　10. B

二、介词填空

1. on/upon/after	2. to	3. on, out	4. at	5. As per, in
6. with	7. for, against	8. into, to	9. of, without	10. for, as

三、非谓语动词

[真题在线]

一、单项选择题

1. B　2. B　3. C　4. C　5. C　6. D

二、翻译下列句子或短语

1. urge sb. to do sth.

2. In order to avoid subsequent amendment, please make sure the stipulations of L/C are in accordance with terms and conditions of the contract.

3. In order to encourage our business, we are willing to provide you with a 5% special discount of the total amount.

4. We are pleased to receive your mail of Oct. 6.

[强化练习]

一、用所给词的正确形式填空

1. to import	2. means	3. to make	4. to compensate
5. having packed	6. adjusted	7. satisfied	8. Aiming

二、单项选择题

1. C　2. B　3. A　4. C　5. C　6. B　7. C　8. D

三、句子翻译

1. To establish an L/C will tie up a lot of our funds.

2. Please make every effort/try your best to have the goods sent within the stipulated time.

3. Please avoid making the same mistake again.

4. We have no choice but to return the damaged goods.

5. To minimize your loss/To reduce your loss to the minimum, we will have this problem solved as soon as possible.

6. The rising/increasing price forced us to raise the price accordingly and we expect to get your understanding.

7. Not wishing to go out from the market, they intend to introduce the new product in June.

8. Having negotiated with suppliers for several times, we finally got the long expected price.

四、句子成分和简单句的五种句型

一、单项选择题

1. D 2. C 3. D 4. B

二、句子翻译

1. We agree to accept all your claims.

2. We could not make any further reduction./ We are unable to reduce the price further.

3. Concerning our standing and reliability，please refer to Bank of China，Hangzhou.

4. The buyer shall file/lodge a claim against the seller by inspection certificate.

一、单项选择题

1. A 2. D 3. C 4. B 5. C 6. C

二、用横线画出句子中的相应成分

1. the full value	2. can be covered	3. Where to find a reliable supplier
4. profitable	5. established	6. S&H Brothers

三、用所给词的正确形式填空

1. informed	2. your	3. Opening/To open	4. sell
5. settling	6. to sign	7. desirous	8. expiry

五、时　态

句子翻译

1. 我们希望你们能在本月底前开立相关信用证。

2. The L/C will reach you in one week or so.

3. If your order is/reaches us not later than the end of this month，we will assure/are sure of /promise the prompt shipment.

4. Considering timely delivery in time，we have to inform you that the goods against Order No. 238 have been ready for shipment，but we have not yet received relevant L/C.

一、单项选择题

1. D 2. A 3. B 4. C 5. B 6. D 7. D 8. B 9. D

二、句子翻译

1. Your full cooperation will be highly appreciated.

2. After receipt of your complaint letter/After we received your complaint letter，we contacted the shipping

company.

3. Up to now/the moment, we still have not received your explanation for the delay.

4. We trust you will be satisfied with our goods and services.

5. They are now negotiating terms of payment in the meeting/conference room.

6. After both parties had discussed for many times, the seller finally decided to make concession on price.

7. We have been providing goods of high quality at favorable prices.

8. Goods left here three weeks ago and they must have reached port of destination (by now).

六、被动语态

[真题在线]

一、单项选择题

1. A 2. D 3. B 4. C 5. C

二、句子翻译

1. 如果/一旦发生本保险单项下可能引起索赔的损失或损坏,应立即通知本公司或本保险单提及的代理人,或应立即将(损失)通知送达本公司或本保险单提及的代理人。

2. The L/C in your favor stipulated in the contract has been issued by Bank of China, Ningbo.

3. 由于信用证规定的装运日期是4月30日且不能再延长,货物必须不晚于上述日期装运。

[强化练习]

一、单项选择题

1. C 2. C 3. C 4. D 5. A 6. D 7. D 8. B

二、将下列句子的主动语态变为被动语态

1. The leather bags are being checked by a customs officer.

2. The goods must be delivered before the end of this month (by us).

3. Any reply hasn't been received yet by them.

4. Our lowest quotation will be faxed to you soon (by us)./ You will be faxed our lowest quotation soon(by us).

5. Your price was found unrealistic by our clients

6. Will the goods be insured on our behalf (by you)?

三、句子翻译

1. The L/C has been opened/issued by the opening/issuing bank.

2. Where are documents/files kept?

3. The contract is being prepared.

4. The letter must be signed by general manager before it is sent.

5. The seller is requested to deliver the goods not later than Oct.1st.

6. Your required sample/Sample required by you will be sent under separate cover.

7. The goods were so seriously damaged that they cannot be sold.

8. Special discount will be allowed on condition that your order reaches us in two weeks.

七、定语从句

一、单项选择题

B

二、句子翻译

1. 我们再次就这个错误向你方致歉,它一定给你们带来了一些不便。

2. Our usual payment terms are confirmed, irrevocable L/C available by draft at sight for the full amount of the invoice value, which should be opened/issued by the bank acceptable to us.

[强化练习]

一、单项选择题

1. D 2. D 3. C 4. B 5. A 6. C 7. D 8. D

二、在横线处填上合适的介词

1. with 2. of 3. to 4. for 5. from/in 6. with 7. without 8. of

三、句子翻译

1. 已收到你方6月20日的邮件,对此我们表示感谢。

2. 这是我们的最终决定,不会发生改变了。

3. 货物晚于预期时间到达,这给我们造成了很大的不便。

4. 他们建议我们把产品引入到东南亚市场,由于经济发展,那里的需求日渐旺盛。

5. Please contact/approach forwarding agent, who will send trucks to collect goods.

6. Please establish the L/C at your earliest convenience, upon receipt of which we will arrange prompt shipment.

7. The goods arrived in poor condition, for which you should be responsible.

8. The fire accident burned the raw material, which made us suffer from/sustain huge losses.

八、状语从句

[真题在线]

一、单项选择题

B

二、句子翻译

1. 由于这些货物的库存有限,我们建议你方早日下单。

2. 当你们将货物备妥待运,请尽快告知。

3. If the price is attractive and quality (is) satisfactory, we will place an order.

4. 你们的价格如此之高,我们不得不从别处购货。

5. Though/Although we know it will tie up large fund to open/establish the L/C, we have to ask you to pay by L/C since it is our initial/first business/owing to the initial/first business between us.

6. Our cotton bed sheets are selling fast because of the soft and durable material./Our cotton bed sheets

are selling fast because the material is soft and durable

[强化练习]

一、单项选择题

1. D 2. D 3. B 4. C 5. A 6. B 7. C 8. B

二、句子翻译

1. 把货物装进坚固/牢固的木箱里以免在运输途中遭受损坏。

2. 一旦您对任何产品感兴趣,请尽快告知。

3. 我们会继续下单,条件是第一批货使我方客人完全满意。

4. 由于过去数月履约过多,我们不得不遗憾地谢绝贵司订单。

5. Though/Although your order is not large, we would still quote you favorable price.

6. Now that the loss is due to our carelessness, we will definitely settle claims as soon as possible.

7. As per/In compliance with the contract, you should /have to pay 30% of the proceeds before shipment is made/we effect shipment.

8. Art goods in contract No. 008 were so damaged that they cannot be sold.

九、名词性从句

[真题在线]

一、单项选择题

1. B 2. C

二、句子翻译

1. We believe/trust you will agree that our products are of high/superior quality and reasonable price.

2. 请告知你们是否同意。

3. 已发现错误是由于我们一位工作人员的粗心包装造成的。

4. 遗憾地说,它们/这些产品比贵方的样品质量低劣得多。

5. We learn that you are in the market for Chinese textiles.

6. That's why we are the leading supplier in this field.

[强化练习]

一、单项选择题

1. D 2. A 3. B 4. C 5. D 6. D 7. A 8. C

二、句子翻译

1. 不言而喻,额外的保费由买方承担。

2. 请放心,第一批货会按时到达你处。

3. 我们的建议是(货物)分四批等量运输。

4. 市场不久以后看涨的消息被证实有误。

5. We are pleased/glad to inform you that the goods reached us safely this morning.

6. What we need urgently is raw material and skilled workers.

7. It is stipulated in the L/C that transshipment is prohibited.

8. Where to find a reliable supplier is our biggest problem at present.

十、虚拟语气

[真题在线]

翻译句子

1. 如果贵司能订购超过2000件所报价产品,我们会给予12%的折扣。

2. 我方在3月6日的信件中告知/通知贵司,我们想试订购30辆飞鸽自行车。

[强化练习]

一、单项选择题

1. A 2. A 3. B 4. C 5. B 6. B 7. D 8. B

二、句子翻译

1. If you had established the L/C earlier, we would have dispatched the goods.

2. It's proposed that the dispute regarding/on quality (should) be solved immediately.

3. Our desire is that you (should) settle the claim as per/according to the contract.

4. Were you to compare our offer with others, you would find our price reasonable.

5. But for your suggestion, the transaction could not have been concluded so smoothly.

6. In OEM business, it's of great importance that the logo provided by seller (should) be legal.

十一、It 的用法

[真题在线]

一、单项选择题

D

二、句子翻译

1. 如果货物不能准时到达,我们也许会拒绝收货。

2. Please see to it that you will ship the total goods/the total goods will be shipped on or before September 30.

3. 已发现错误是由于我们的工作人员的粗心包装造成的。

4. 如贵方能够航寄一份全套商品目录及一些布料剪样供我们研究,我方将不胜感激。

5. We do hope to establish long-term business relations with your company in the near future.

[强化练习]

一、单项选择题

1. B 2. C 3. A 4. B 5. D 6. B 7. D 8.C

二、句子翻译

1. It's impossible to use FOB to replace CIF in our contract.

2. It's said that S/S "Forever" reached Shanghai last night.

3. I think it convenient to make transshipment via/at Hong Kong.

4. Do you think it necessary to insist on making an offer on FOB?

5. We did make them an offer a/one week ago.

6. It's in this room that the buyer and the seller discussed the price.

7. It's not until this morning that we loaded the goods on board the ship.

8. It's due to/owing to our good relations that we allow you an accommodation this time.

十二、省　略

[真题在线]

句子翻译

1. If interested, please contact us.

2. We're pleased to receive your inquiring of Apr. 10.

3. Looking forward to your reply.

4. Shipping marks: To be designed by the seller.

[强化练习]

一、单项选择题

1. C　2. A　3. D　4. C　5. D　6. B　7. C　8. D

二、句子翻译

1. Shipment: Not later than July 21.

2. We are now enclosing a copy of e-catalog.

3. When/while counting, please be careful.

4. If necessary, we will contact the shipping company.

5. 关于我方资信,请向我们的开户行——宁波银行查询。

6. 我们的产品由上好的材料制成,在东欧国家畅销。

7. 在检查货物时,我们注意到其中的一些损坏了。

8. 尽管受到邀请,他们还是不会参加交易会。

商函写作篇

一、信函格式

[真题在线]

Dear Sirs,

Thank you for your quotation of March 30 together with the samples. We find both the quality and prices are up to our expectations. We are pleased to place an order with you according to the following terms and conditions:

Name of Commodity：Chinese costumes（garments）for ladies

Fabric Content：100% silk

Quantity：10,000 pieces, with 5% more or less at the seller's option

Unit price：EUR 98.00/pc, CIF Hamburg, Germany

Total value(Total amount)：EUR 980,000.00

Packing：100 pieces packed in a case/each case containing 100 pieces/100 pieces per case

Time of Shipment：Not later than May 30, 2016

Port of Shipment(Port of Loading)：Ningbo, China

Port of Destination：Hamburg, Germany

Shipping Marks：To be designed by the seller

Terms of Payment：By 100% irrevocable sight L/C to reach the seller before May 10, 2016 and valid for negotiation in china until the 15th day(within 15 days) after the date of shipment.

We are looking forward to your confirmation of our order.

Yours faithfully,

[强化练习]

1.

Dear Sirs,

We are pleased to receive your enquiry letter.

We are now writing to inform you that we are one of the leading manufacturers of electric fans with 58 years' experience. Our goods are famous for their high quality and prompt delivery. They are superior to other products in quality and price.

Enclosed please find our latest catalog with price list and sample book. If your order exceeds 2,000 sets, we are prepared to allow you a 10% discount. We are sure that you will find our goods (are) good value for money.

Looking forward to your early reply.

Yours sincerely,

2.

Dear Sirs,

Re：Men's Shirts Art. No. 258

We have received your email of June18 with thanks.

Our price for men's shirts is fixed on a reasonable level and it is difficult (for us) to give you any discount. Regarding this offer, you can refer to other suppliers. To be frank, we have quoted you our most favorable price. Besides/In addition, the price for raw material is/has been on the rise. We expect/hope you can understand our position. In view of our past friendly cooperative relations, we are prepared to allow you a 3% quantity discount.

Looking forward to your careful consideration of our suggestion/proposal and please send us your early confirmation by fax.

Yours sincerely,

二、句子翻译

句子翻译

1. Our leather products enjoy high reputation both at home and abroad.

2. We're interested to purchase/in purchasing Men's Shirts Item No. MS1201.

3. We have received your e-mail of May 5th with thanks.

4. There is a strong demand in the market.

5. Thanks to/owing to mutual effort，we were able to conclude the transaction successfully/smoothly.

6. This low price/offer leaves us with narrow margin of profit/profit margin.

[强化练习]

一、句子翻译

1. Samples will be sent under separate cover.

2. We are sorry that we cannot accept your counter-offer.

3. We strongly/firmly believe（that）our products are good value for money.

4. The complete catalog together with the required/needed sample was sent this morning.

5. If the first order is smoothly executed，we will consider repeating an order for 2,000 cans.

6. As we are in urgent need of the ordered goods，please make prompt delivery.

7. L/C DC005 is in favor of DBC Corporation.

8. As a result of shortage/lack of raw material，the prices of products rise sharply. /As there is a shortage/lack of raw material，the prices of products rise sharply.

二、改错（找出句子的一处错误并改正）

1. C（is→are）

2. B（over→is over; over→exceeds）

3. C（validity→valid）

4. D（this→these）

5. A（删除 be）

6. C（删除 but）或 A（删除 Much as）